GUERRILLA

MEDIA

BUYING

FOR SMALL (AND LARGE) BUSINESS

Discover How David Beat Goliath in Business

Get More Ad Exposure per Dollar Spent

Increase Share of Voice
Get More Customers
Increase Share of Market
Improve Profitability

Ronald D. Geskey

2020:Marketing Communications LLC

2020:Marketing Communications LLC

Guerilla Media Buying
for Small (and Large) Business
Discover How David Beat Goliath in Business

Author: Ronald D. Geskey, Sr,
COPYRIGHT © 2010 BY RONALD D. GESKEY,
2020:MARKETING COMMUNICATIONS LLC

ISBN 10: 1450598765   ISBN 13: 9781450598767

Disclaimer

This publication is designed to provide accurate and authoritative information. It is sold with the understanding that the publisher is not engaged in rendering legal, accounting, or other professional services. If legal advice or other expert assistance is required, the services of a competent professional should be sought.

GUERRILLA MEDIA BUYING

FOR SMALL (AND LARGE) BUSINESS

**Discover How David Beat Goliath in Business
Get More Ad Exposure per Dollar Spent**

*Increase Share of Voice
Increase Customers
Increase Share of Market
Improve Profitability*

Ronald D. Geskey, Sr.

Published by
2020:Marketing Communications LLC
P.O. 82476
Rochester, MI48308
Email: marketing2020@aol.com

4

About the Author

Ronald D. Geskey, Sr. has over 30 years of senior management experience in account management, marketing and media planning and buying at some of the best advertising agencies in the country, including Leo Burnett/Chicago, D'Arcy, Campbell-Ewald/Detroit, and General Motors R*Works.

Ron has worked with very large corporations as well as small businesses, and he has a unique perspective on how small businesses can not only survive, but win against the Goliaths because he understands their weaknesses.

Geskey has also taught marketing, advertising, and media at several major universities.

Ron has a master's degree from Southern Illinois University, doctoral work at Texas Tech University, as well as additional post-graduate professional education from Northwestern, Wharton, and Michigan State University.

He is the author of many marketing and media publications, including the *Thumbnail Media Planner; David vs. Goliath, Free Marketing in Social Media: 500 Tactics and Best Practices, The 10 Immutable Laws of Buying Broadcast Media; Media 101, Strategic Media Planning; Recency Planning: Revisited; Effective Reach: Revisited*; and many others.

Ron is married with two sons, one who works in the ad biz, the other an attorney. And he is a very proud grandfather!

Acknowledgments

This book is dedicated to my fantastic wife of 40 years, Caroline. I thank her for her patience and support during our marriage, and for her encouragement to write this book. Without her encouragement to share what I have learned to (hopefully) help others, this book probably would not have been written.

I would also like to thank my sons, Ron, Jr. and Stephen, for their encouragement and support. I am very proud of both of them for what they have accomplished and especially for the fine young adults they have become.

I have also been extremely fortunate to have had some great mentors over the years, without whom it's hard to know what might have happened to me. Dr. Don Hileman and Dr. George Brown nurtured me through college and helped me land my first big job. Then Linc Bumba mentored me and put me on a career success track in my first real job at Leo Burnett in Chicago.

To these colleagues and the many others who have taught me and mentored me over the years, I am extremely appreciative

.

On Advertising

"Early to bed, early to rise,

work like hell, and advertise."

--Laurence Peters,
1919-1990
Canadian Writer & Teacher

Table of Contents

Preface

How can a small business ever hope to compete with a large corporation?

Like the mythical battle where David took down Goliath, this book provides small (and large) business owners and managers with a practical and tested weapon they can use to more effectively compete with larger businesses—who may   enjoy higher awareness, more favorable perceptions, and higher purchase consideration.

*Your weapon to compete with these Goliaths is **Guerrilla Media Buying**. If you learn and use the techniques found in this book, you will discover how to beat Goliath in business!*

Perception is Reality

When you think about it, ***perception is reality*** to consumers.

Perceptions drive purchase decisions, to buy or not to buy. Yet, consumer perceptions about businesses and products are affected by many things, rational and emotional-- personal experience with the product or service (even an ancient experience), word out mouth received from family members and friends, awareness and attitudes toward   competitive offerings, perceptions of quality, pricing and value, as well as advertising as well as all forms of marketing communications shaping the brand experience.

Perceptions caused by advertising result from the messages seen or heard-- and *how often and where those messages are seen.*

It is very difficult to change perceptions and beliefs, especially when they are deeply ingrained, based on old information no longer consistent with the facts.

For example, even after General Motors improved vehicle quality to rival the Japanese vehicles, most people still thought GM products were lower in quality, reliability, and durability than Japanese products. So consumers continued not to buy GM products and GM's share continued declining until the US government takeover.

This book is about Guerrilla Media Buying, a technique which can help change consumer perceptions in your favor.

Introduction to Media Buying

Every business that advertises buys media. Some, no doubt, do a great job of getting high value for their budgets, while others waste their money. It may or may not have ever occurred to you that the effectiveness with which you make your media investments has a huge effect on your marketplace results and Return on Investment (ROI). Media can even have a dramatic effect on consumer perceptions and purchase behavior. (That's why I wrote this book.)

What is Media Buying?

Media buying involves selecting and negotiating the purchase of advertising time and space in media vehicles—programs on television and radio networks or stations, magazines and newspapers, a variety of internet options, outdoor and event sponsorships, and many more.

For example, every time a commercial runs on television, somebody had to first decide that the program reaches the advertiser's target audience, that advertising in the program would be cost effective, and somebody had to actually negotiate with the purchase with the seller (network or local station). The buyer of the :30 second spot in the program had to negotiate the price of the spot-- as well as where the commercial would be positioned within the program and what the seller would to extend the impact of the buy.

Success Based on Win-Win

In any competitive business situation, there should only be winners. *winners and losers.* That applies to those making the decisions on media selection, buying and negotiating. Media buys are win-win when both the buyer and seller benefit from making a deal. For example, the buyer may award a particular seller the lion's share of the budget in exchange for some deep discounts in pricing and value added elements.

Have you ever thought about the business implications of planning and negotiating your media buys? Maybe not, if you're like a lot of smaller (and many larger) advertisers. But consider this typical scenario:

Advertiser A buys an advertising media schedule of TV and Radio spots and newspaper ads that reach 500,000 people at a cost of $50,000. Advertiser B buys a very similar media schedule—which reaches 450,000 people for $40,000. A third competitor—Advertiser C-- puts together a diversified communications schedule using different media that reach 1,000,000 people for $25,000.

Advertiser C is a *Guerrilla Media Buyer*. He/she didn't just buy advertising, but when he did, he got 50%+ more for his money. Advertiser C also capitalized on a lot of free and low cost communication ideas-- which dollar for dollar-- had more impact than traditional advertising alone.

So, if you had a choice, which advertiser would you want to emulate?

The Stakes

The media buying stakes are high. Companies and organizations spend hundreds of billions of dollars annually in advertising media and other marketing communications venues. The waste factor is huge.

The problem is that many companies spend their advertising and marketing budgets inefficiently and ineffectively. This is a particular problem for many smaller business owners who do not have the time or necessarily the expertise to create the best plans or to negotiate the best possible media buys with sellers of time and space and promotions. Also, the agencies employed by some companies also lack the knowledge and skills to get the most bang for your buck.

For example, a firm with a $100,000 budget can receive market impact worth $50,000 or $300,000, depending on media buying effectiveness.

Buying advertising media or promotions or other marketing programs is nothing like buying merchandise or services for a small business. But the skills must be mastered to move the business forward. This book will help you acquire those skills.

As Yogi Berra once said about baseball also applies to media, "If it was easy, everybody would be doing it."

Buying media— whether it's broadcast time, newspaper or magazine space, or internet key word search ads-- requires a great deal of information, knowledge and skill. As evidence of that, top media professionals in larger firms make salaries of hundreds of thousands of dollars per year.

The fact that so many firms spend their advertising and marketing budgets so inefficiently or ineffectively presents a real business building opportunity for those who learn the ropes and translate it to action.

Purpose of Book

The purpose of this book is to coach you in learning how to practice the art and science of Guerrilla Media Buying. In this book, you will learn what is important to become a successful Guerrilla Media Buyer even if you are currently a newbie. For example, you will learn:

- About important media concepts and terminology you can use to knowledgably communicate with media sales people.

- Enough media math to be able to analyze alternative media buys, and to be able to determine if a proposal makes any sense.

- About the marketing foundation necessary as a prerequisite to media buying.

- How to select the right forms of marketing communications to most cosdt effectively address your marketing tasks.

- How to evaluate analyze and evaluate alternative media options in order to select the most cost effective e ones.

- How to negotiate traditional media buys at the lowest possible prices.

- How to drive your costs down and effectiveness up by using non traditional and alternative media.

- How to use a variety of non traditional media buying techniques to help improve overall cost efficiencies.

***

On the Art of Battle

...the general who wins a battle makes many calculations in his temple ere the battle is fought. The general who loses a battle makes but few calculations beforehand. Thus do many calculations lead to victory, and few calculations to defeat: how much more no calculation at all! It is by attention to this point that I can foresee who is likely to win or lose.

-Sun Tzu, the Art of War

Chapter 1
Introduction to Guerrilla Media Buying

Guerrilla Media Buying *is an "unconventional" system of planning and buying media communications opportunities-- that relies on time, energy and imagination-- rather than a big fat marketing budget.*

But unconventional doesn't mean stupid.

There are some who believe that guerrilla marketing warfare of any type means that you just need to go out and do cool stuff, and that little homework, research, discipline and thought are needed... ***Just do it...*** *like the Nike commercial says. Yet as the great Chinese warrior, Sun Tzu said in* ***The Art of War****, "... many calculations lead to victory, and few calculations to defeat..."*

So guerrilla media buying isn't about just going out and doing and buying media that you personally like. It is extremely important that you do your homework and planning prior to launching a guerrilla media campaign.

Be Smart, Do Your Homework.

Guerrilla media planning and buying have a different focus than traditional media buying. In traditional buying, the advertiser or media buyer would almost automatically call the stations and place orders for some spots proposed by the sales reps. The guerrilla buyer also may use traditional media, but much more selectively and more cost effectively. The Guerrilla Buyer may also turn to some low cost, creative and nontraditional media to increase audience delivery, effectiveness, and cost efficiency, and, hopefully. ROI.

Why Is Guerrilla Media Important?

Why is it so important to increase the amount of your communication with consumers while reducing out of pocket costs? Think about it like this:

If you were in the market for a new HD television set, what store would you think of (to shop at) first? If you needed a new suit, what store would come to mind first? If you needed some premium frozen vegetables to serve your guests Saturday night, what brand first comes to mind?

If you decided to go ahead and buy that new luxury car, what one model would come to mind first? Which car dealer? Which computer? Your answers represent one of the most important and analyzed metrics in marketing.

Your answers to these questions represent the Share of Mind (also known as Top of Mind Awareness) each brand or store enjoys with you in different categories. It is easy to understand why top of mind awareness is so highly correlated with share of market.

In part, the question becomes one of how to cost effectively increase Top of Mind Awareness. The simple answer is to raise Top of Mind Awareness efficiently by dramatically increasing Share of Voice without incremental marketing expense/spend

How to Compete With Larger Competitors

This book is about using guerrilla media buying techniques to more effectively compete against larger competitors who have larger budgets, financial and organizational resources behind them.

The *Winning Formula* is simple: *Dramatically increase your Share of Voice and Quality of Voice—by 50 percent or more— without increasing your marketing/advertising budget.* That one accomplishment will drive greater sales and market share with enhanced profit margins. (You can put your incremental profit in the bank or reinvest it in more media for even greater Share of Voice, market share, and profit.)

What is Share of Voice (SOV)?

Share of Voice (SOV) is simply your business's or brand's percentage (share) of total advertising/communications messages (usually measured as spending) in your primary business category and geographic marketing area. For example, if you spend $100,000 in your market area on advertising and your competitors spend another $900,000, total spending in your category equals $1,000,000. Your $100,000 investment represents 10% of the total. In other words, **your SOV is 10%.**

Therefore, your SOV is roughly determined by the size of your ad budget compared to the collective ad budgets of your competitors. Bottom line: It's easy to increase top-of-mind awareness if you just increase your budget (and spend the money wisely).

Share of Voice vs. Share of Market

Why is SOV important? According to John Davis, author of *Magic Numbers for Consumer Marketing*, SOV is vital. His rationale: "Advertising does have an influence on perception and a high share of voice can lead to an increased awareness, which ultimately can lead to increased sales and market share."

As shown in the following diagram, a substantial body of research has found that SOV leads to Share of Mind (Top of Mind Awareness), which leads to Share of Market. In other words, all else being equal, if you increase SOV enough, increased share of market should follow.

Share of Voice vs. Share of Market

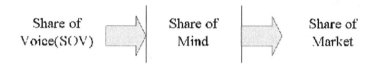

Share of Voice(SOV) → Share of Mind → Share of Market

Historically, there has always been a strong, documented, and measured relationship between SOV and Share of Market. It is a very strong correlation, not a perfect 1:1, but it is close.

A.C. Nielsen, a large market research company that tracks sales and share for consumer products, has historically tracked the sales and market share performance of new products in relation to share of voice. Nielsen concluded that SOV most often led the attained Share of Market by 40-100+ percent over an 18-month period. In other words, a new product that achieved a 20% share of market in its category accomplished it at least partly due to a 30-40% SOV during the 18 month introductory period.

Consider the introduction of Japanese import vehicles into the U.S. market. Initially with low quality perceptions, Japanese brands like Toyota greatly improved their product quality and also supported a SOV far in excess of their market share. Over the years we have seen how their strategy paid off as many Americans still perceive Japanese vehicle quality as better than "American made" vehicles.

It was also found that, in general, SOV and Share of Market are often very similar numbers, leading to the conclusion that market share would more likely be maintained when share of voice at least equals share of market and <u>increased</u> when share of voice significantly leads share of market.

Other companies and advertising agencies have also conducted research on the relationship between SOV and share of market and have found high correlations.

Obviously, there are exceptions to the rule—SOV is obviously not the only factor impacting market share. Sometimes the relationship and correlation is not automatic. If the creative message or price, or the product, or customer service is not in lock step with what the consumer wants and expects, SOV might not help much in the long term. But all else being equal, SOV can be an important and documented business-building tool.

How Do You Measure SOV?

If your company is large enough, your ad spending and your competitors' ad spending is probably compiled by syndicated media research companies. If so, you can gather spending information for all competitors on a regular (quarterly and/or annual) basis, and you can easily calculate each competitor's percentage of the aggregated total spend to estimate SOV for each.

More likely, if you are a small company, there is no existing research report to give you the competitive media expenditure data you need to calculate and trend SOV for your company and your key competitors.

So, the bad news: to get the data, you have to call each of the relevant media and ask them how much each competitor spent in their media vehicle in your marketing area in a certain time frame. (You may have to guesstimate some data yourself.) When you have all the data compiled, add up the total expenditures by competitor by medium and calculate each company's share of the grand total expenditures.

Our experience has been that most media are cooperative in responding to such requests, especially if you are a customer. (Also, remember, your competitors may be asking the same questions!)

How to Increase SOV

If *increased* SOV is a precursor to increased market share, it is important to understand a small business' options for growing its SOV:

1. Increase your marketing/advertising budget significantly (e.g., 50-100%++): may not be profitable.

2. Form an in-house agency to buy media. Collect the 15 per cent agency commission and cash discount on qualifying media buys. Most media have a 15% commission for agencies built into their rates. Plus you can often get a 2% cash discount if you pay within 10 days. Reinvest savings into SOV! A small step in the right direction.

3. Increase "Effective SOV" by eliminating waste in current ad spending. Reinvest "savings." Duh!

4. Become a Guerrilla Media Buyer to generate even greater impact but without additional investment! Yes!

Quality of Voice

Quality of Voice (QOV) is the creative quality and effectiveness of the advertiser's communications message and ads. Is the message right? Is it executed powerfully? Is the target right? Is the creative message effective in persuading consumers? *Do the ads and commercials and stories make the business look important, successful and credible? QOV is about image management.*

Many small businesses (needing to spend frugally) skimp far too much on the quality of their creative. But consumers form their impressions and image of a business partly by the ads and messages you put out there.

You would never make a personal sales call to IBM executives without a recent haircut and wearing your favorite dirty, tattered jeans. So, why would anybody put ads in front of the public which look like they came from a second or third class company? All of your communications must give consumers the impression that you are an important, successful, quality company that they should consider doing business with.

If you need creative assistance, but don't use an advertising agency, you can still get help from many talented freelancers (e.g., see Guru.com).

Effective Share of Voice (ESOV)

Is creative really all that matters? No, of course not. Are gross advertising expenditures a good measure of *ESOV*? The answer, of course, is NO, because from the consumer's perspective, SOV and Quality of Voice are inter-related. In forming more positive consumer perceptions among more consumers, ESOV is the result of both a quantitative share of messages/dollars and the quality of those messages.

Quality of Voice is qualitative but crucial. Achieving high Quality of Voice requires that there is a strong, strategic marketing foundation in place, that the target market is properly defined, that the message is right, the creative is powerful, and the media plan is impactful. ESOV is the result of both the quantity and quality of messages, i.e.:

SOV + QOV = ESOV

From a media standpoint, advertisers achieve different levels of efficiencies in their planning and buying, impact, and audience and communication value for their media investments. One company might spend their budget with 110% effectiveness, while another might spend at only 30 percent effectiveness. Why? Because they made either smart or really bad media decisions. And perhaps they were taken to the cleaners during negotiations by smart media sellers, when the buyer was simply not prepared for a winning negotiation.

However, it is likely that you can increase your ESOV in your market area by 50-100 percent or more without increasing your ad budget by one dime.

As non technically as possible, this book will teach you how to leverage your budget to get more bang for the buck, while removing waste from your current advertising media spending.

A large portion of a budget can be wasted when a media strategy and plan are out of synch with the consumer, when marketing problems are ill-defined or communications objectives are too vague all the result of a flawed planning process. *What if a smarter marketing plan could increase the consumer impact of communications by 50 - 100% or more?*

Net: If smarter planning and smarter buying could increase your effective media exposure by just 100%, that would be like doubling your budget…but without spending one additional dime!

Should You Cut Advertising in a Recession?

This above discussion also relates directly to the timely issue of advertising during a recession, like the one experienced from 2008 - 2010 or beyond. With high unemployment and nervous consumers, there are fewer customers. This causes lower sales and profit margins. Every company has to decide what strategy to follow in terms of advertising during tough times.

Many advertisers/marketers understandably cut their ad spending during an economic downturn. Other advertisers maintain or even increase their spending during recessions. The good news goes to those to hang in there, because they often emerge from the recession with a higher market share than they had prior to the recession. Short term pain for long term gain.

But consumers don't know what you spend (and could care less). So what if you could maintain or increase your advertising communication levels, while simultaneously reducing your spending? If you can accomplish that, you might be able to increase your market share, reduce expenses, and improve profitability in a tough economy.

***

If you learn and implement what this book teaches, your Effective Share of Voice will grow, and increased market share will likely follow, provided that your business is otherwise on track. If it doesn't, you will know you have other problems that need to be fixed so that your increased SOV can work for you!

Very simply, increasing your SOV without increasing ad spending is a cost effective way to defeat the Goliaths in your industry. It won't be easy, but it will probably be a lot easier and cheaper than the alternatives.

All else being equal, maintaining SOV will help to maintain your market share, while increasing your ESOV—even without raising your budget—should help you achieve greater market share and profitability.

Chapter 1
Review

1. What is Share of Voice (SOV)?

2. What is the relationship between Share of Voice and Share of Market?

3. What is the difference between SOV and ESOV as described in this book?

4. What is *your* SOV vs. competitors in your business category & geographic market area?

	$ Spend	% Total
Your Company		
Competitor A		
Competitor B		
Others		
Total		100.0

5. List the media you have to contact to generate the data for your SOV analysis (TV & radio stations, newspapers, magazines, trade publications, outdoor companies, etc.) Record the data.

6. What is Quality of Voice? How important is it?

7. Think of several examples of really bad creative for a smaller (or larger) business. How do you think consumers would describe and react to it?

8. Do an honest assessment of your past media buying practices and results. What have you learned?

CAVEAT EMPTOR: LET THE MEDIA BUYER BEWARE

Chapter 2
Caveat Emptor:
Let the Media Buyer Beware

*"I know that half of my advertising dollars are wasted,
I just don't know which half."*

--John Wanamaker

John Wannamaker, who was the CEO of a Nordstrom department store equivalent in the late 1800s, was in a meeting with his banker, a Rockefeller. During the meeting, Wanamaker uttered his now famous quote, "I know that half of my advertising is wasted, I just don't know which half."

Today, the dirty little secret is that little has changed—except that some experts believe that advertisers are now squandering 80-90% of their advertising budgets. This waste should not be tolerable to anyone trying to build a business, especially a small business. The good news is, if you are willing and able to learn the mysteries of media, you can identify and eliminate the majority of spending waste-- because it is human caused.

Replace the wasted spending with a cost-effective plan and more effective negotiations of your media buys, and you will increase ESOV

Caveat Emptor

Let the Buyer Beware.

Ignorance of media is no excuse.

Advertising media sales are a highly competitive $300 billion business with over 50,000 media vehicles and many thousands of media sales reps competing for business. No place for media buying newbies, you might argue, but there are plenty of newbies making multi-million decisions about where, when, and how to spend billions of dollars of your money and others' money.

Caveat Emptor, says the law. Just like advertisers can use a little puffery in their ads ("This is the greatest product ever!"), media sellers also use puffery. Like advertisers, however, they may not misrepresent the facts or lie. But media are not liable for dumb decisions by the buyer or for buyer remorse. The buyer has a responsibility to make prudent buying decisions.

Caveat Emptor is a very good reminder, especially to those who are newly involved in making important media decisions and negotiating media purchases.

As mentioned above, there are perhaps 50,000 media vehicles trying to sell advertising (many created only for that purpose). There are millions or billions of bytes of research information on audience sizes, demographics, psychographics, commercial audience, ad exposure scores, in home and out of home reading, viewing in public places, recall and communications scores, cross tabs of everything, cost efficiency rankers, macro media usage studies, media impact studies, and so on. There are literally thousands of studies, and there are thousands of people compiling media data and sales pitches and making sales presentations.

There is so much research conducted on media audiences and media effectiveness that no one has been able to integrate and utilize it all.

And everybody, agencies and media, creatively manipulate existing data to prove their points.

There are hundreds of thousands of sales calls made expressly for the purpose of selling ads in all of these media. Plus there are baseball games, lunches, dinners, and cocktail parties, all with the same purpose... selling ads.

Caveat Emptor: remember, every media pitch will show you how that media vehicle is number one in something—and why it is the best media buy on the planet for you. *Caveat Emptor*. Do your own careful analysis of the <u>facts</u>.

How Ad Dollars Get Wasted

There are hundreds, maybe thousands, of ways to waste or diminish the effectiveness of a small business's advertising budget. Waste might result from not having a sound overall marketing strategy or a weak positioning that doesn't strike a chord with the target consumer.

> *A bad strategy cannot be made into an effective strategy by pouring more money behind a bad idea.*

Or, waste might result from weak advertising creative—ads that are either focused on communicating the wrong messages—or ads that are just poorly executed, or the production is so amateurish that the business takes on the image of "Cousin Fred's." Then the advertising goes unnoticed or is even detrimental to image of the advertiser.

IMPORTANT: Do not chince on your creative. You have to look like you are a legitimate alternative to Goliath! Plus, more exposure of advertising that harms your image makes your marketing situation worse, not better.

A lot of advertising budget waste can be traced back to poor planning, bad media strategy and wasteful media buying by uneducated buyers.

CAVEAT EMPTOR: LET THE MEDIA BUYER BEWARE

*While everyone thinks he or she is an creative or media genius,
ignorance and arrogance will surely waste the budget.*

Consider these examples of costly waste:

Example 1: Take the case (true story) of the board of directors of a large automotive dealer group in a major market. Emotionally, the dealers felt connected to a local pro sports team—plus they liked the idea of getting free tickets to the games. When their sponsorship was up for renewal, their advertising agency evaluated the audience and promotional value of the station's proposal, finding the actual dollar value to be about $150,000. The station was upside down in rights fees they had to pay the team, and knowing that the dealers would pay most any price, the station would not sell the sponsorship for less than $550,000.

The Board of Directors decided to buy the sponsorship anyway, valued at $150,000, for $550,000, effectively wasting $400,000 of the dealers' money (70% of the total), which could have been used instead to produce another $3.2 million in gross profit.

Another way of looking at the issue: Would you pay $100 per share for a stock selling at $25 per share? What is the difference?

The moral of the story is that media decisions are important financial decisions, not unlike buying the right piece of technology for your business. But if media decisions like this one are made emotionally--rather than careful considerations and the cold, hard facts, costly mistakes will occur—which reduces the amount of advertising exposure you can buy—which in turn reduces your share of voice, sales, market share, and profits.

Example 2: With their deep pockets, Anheuser-Bush and the auto companies can buy as many $2.6 million dollar 30-second spots in the Super Bowl as they want (A-B recently had 10). From a comparative cost efficiency standpoint, these spots are only worth about $800,000 each. That works out to about 70% waste—$1.8 million per spot or $18 million total in AB's case.

Why? Because to survive, small businesses must transform into lean, mean media machines. In contrast, many giants' budgets are apparently larger than they actually need, and they are prone to buy certain media properties regardless of price. (Unfortunately, the stockholders pay the price for corporate waste without even realizing it.)

There are hundreds of ways to waste ad dollars in the media planning and buying process. Here are a few more examples:

- Marketing problem poorly defined.
- Wrong type of communications used in an ambiguous situation
- The target market is incorrectly defined
- The selected advertising media miss the target market
- Advertising dollars are largely spent outside the primary marketing area
- Inefficient media buys, media priced too high for audience and value received
- Timing of advertising is wrong
- Media are efficient on paper, but not effective when you look below the surface at communications factors
- Ineffective and/or immature negotiations with media sellers
- Lack of the right information about the media audiences
- Lack of information/intelligence on market conditions
- Underutilization of non traditional media
- Lack of understanding of media strengths and weaknesses from a communications perspective
- Under-utilization of guerilla media-buying techniques
- Confusion about whether to employ Recency or Effective Reach planning philosophies
- Media buyers lack the media effectiveness information they need to make the right buys
- Media are purchased for emotional rather than rational reasons
- Many others…but you get the idea!

If your objective is to increase market share via ESOV, your options are: to 1) increase your budget or 2) increase your media efficiency and effectiveness. Increasing your ESOV by 50% - 300% is the same as increasing your advertising budget by 50% or 100% or more!!

What would a 50-100% increase in advertising do for *your sales?* What would that sales increase in do for your *profits*—if it was achieved without any incremental advertising investment?

Some Fundamentals

To improve advertising and media effectiveness, we must first know the answer to some fundamental questions such as:

* Who are our best prospects? (Demographics, life style, etc.)

* Where are these prospects located? (market areas, zips, etc.)

* When is the best time to communicate with them?

* Why do they buy from one business but not another?

* What motivates these buyers (such as quality, value, time, etc.)?

* What is their media behavior, and how can we most effectively communicate with them?

* What are the company's marketing objectives, strategies, problems and opportunities?

Messages & Media

At the core, every advertising plan consists of two basic components: messages and media. Messages are the ads and commercials, often created and produced by an advertising agency's creative department, which are intended to ultimately persuade a target audience to buy a firm's products or services. But those messages have to first be seen or heard—i.e., delivered to those consumers who might buy the product or service.

Media are the channels of communication—the vehicles used to deliver those advertising messages (ads and commercials)—to some defined audience or audiences.

If the target audience is poorly defined, you may select the wrong media. Or you can select the wrong media to reach the right audience.

Role of Media Today

The role of media planning and buying is to most cost effectively expose the company/brand's advertising or other marketing communications messages to *the right people in the right place, at the right time, and with maximum communications impact.* If you can do this, you will help maximize the return on investment we receive from our communications investments.

The term *media* is the generic, plural term applied to all media or to a class of media. For example, television, radio, magazines, newspapers, and the internet are *media*. The term *medium*, on the other hand, refers to a single class of media. Television is an advertising medium, radio is an advertising medium.

Media vehicles are the specific media carriers chosen within a class of media to deliver the messages to the target audience. For example, *Time* and *Newsweek* are media vehicles within the class of magazines. The "Today Show" and "Good Morning America" are television media vehicles. WXYZ-Radio station is a radio media vehicle.

Media Planning

Some people just think that media is just about buying or negotiating a "media buy." But long before there is any buying of media, a strategic media plan must be developed that addresses the company's marketing needs, problems and opportunities.

After we are sure we have the right plan, *then* we need to buy the right media at the right time, place, and price to execute the strategic media plan.

Media Planning is the *process* that media planners go through in order to develop the most effective media plan, and which will provide the advertiser with the best possible ROI.

Because of the proliferation of so many new media and technologies, there are more media choices than ever. This is driving a "new" kind of integrated communications planning as shown in the following diagram which shows many alternatives to automatically using advertising. Are you generating all of the free publicity you should? Do you need for people to see, touch, and feel or sample your product at an event?

The New Media Planning:
Integrated Marketing Communications

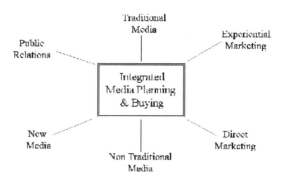

The "practice" of media is both an art and a science. Media at least tries to apply science to the planning and buying processes. As you will discover, as you become hands on, there is voluminous media audience data, effectiveness research, and computer models to assist media people in their quest for greater and greater effectiveness. However, as important as it is, the data and computer assists are imperfect tools. And as media options increase, it will be even more important to ensure that the media plan is based on the best marketing information, media insights, logic, and creativity available.

What is a Media Plan?

A media plan is the action plan describing in detail how, when, where and why the advertising messages will be delivered to the target audience. It's a total plan about everything you're going to do to impact the consumer with exposures of your advertising messages. It has four parts:

- Situation Analysis
- Media Objectives
- Media Strategy
- Media Tactics

1. Situation Analysis - The situation analysis contains the marketing and business background and facts needed to develop a sound media strategy and plan, e.g.:

- Market & industry data
- Target audience data
- Competitive information
- Geographic sales data
- Seasonal sales data
- Marketing problems & opportunities
- Marketing and sales objectives
- Advertising Objectives & Priorities, e.g., awareness of store, awareness of merchandise assortments, image, etc.

2. Media Objectives - Based on the marketing situation, the next step in the planning process is to develop a set of objectives for the media plan—a set of guidelines for the exposure of advertising or other messages to the target markets. Objectives define what is to be accomplished, e.g.:

- Overall Communications Objective
- Target Audience Definition
- Exposure Goals
- Geographic Priorities
- Timing Priorities

* Communication Goals

3. Media Strategy - Given the media objectives, the next step is to formulate the most effective possible strategy for addressing the objectives. Strategy spells out how to accomplish the objectives, e.g.:

* Media & Communications Mix/Rationale
* Spending/Budget Strategy
* Geographic Weighting/Use of Media
* Scheduling of Media
* Other Strategies

5. **Tactical Plan** - The tactical plan details all of the media vehicles chosen, the months, weeks, or even time of day the advertising will appear in the media vehicles, and what markets, including national or individual, local markets or neighborhoods. Following is a simplified example of what a media plan might look like on a flow chart/schedule. Note: Normally TRP levels, ad configurations and other key information would be included on the flow chart.

Example of Media Plan Flowchart

	2008											
	JANUARY								MARCH			
	29	5	12	19	26	2	9	16	23	1	8	15	22
LOCAL CABLE TV												
Entertainment					17	17	17	17	17	17	17	17	17
Sports	0	0	0	0	6	6	6	6	6	6	6	6	6
News					3	3	3	3	3	3	3	3	3
Latenight	23	23	23	23	23	23	23	23	23	23	23	23	23
DIRECT MAIL												
NEWSPAPER (NEWS)												

What is Media Buying?

After the media plan has been developed and approved by the advertiser, the plan must be executed. The time and space must be "bought" so that the ads and commercials actually run and reach the target audience.

Buying time on television, radio, or the internet usually involves a fairly lengthy negotiation with the sellers (networks or stations) in order to get the lowest possible price/highest quality for the time periods, programs, and commercial positions that best meet the advertiser's needs. This is true regardless of whether the buy is on a big national network (ABC, CBS, NBC, FOX) or on a local TV or radio station in Columbia, South Carolina.

Buying space in the print media usually does not require as much negotiation, although it can. Print media like to work from their "rate cards," specifying the rate they want for a space unit and what discounts they offer for a certain level of expenditure or ad frequency. But the world is changing, and print media are increasingly willing to negotiate their pricing and other value added offerings in exchange for a certain budget commitment.

The Business of Media

Marketing Communications Spend (MARCOM)

Marketing communications is big business. In 2008, an estimated $778 billion was spent in the USA on advertising and promotion, while promotion remained the dominant form with 69% of total spend:

	2008 Billions	% Total	% Ch.
Advertising	$246*	31%	+6
Promotion	$529*	69%	+6
Public Relations	$4	1%	+6
Total	$775	100%	+6

*Direct marketing ad dollars included in promotion.   Source: Jack Myer

Advertising Media Expenditures

A $248 billion industry, media spending grew only 5% in 2009 vs. 2002. However, as shown in the following table, there were some media winners and losers during the same period.

The big winners included the internet (note: online dollars do not include search), outdoor and direct mail.

The big losers include radio, magazines, and newspapers, if current trends were taken into account. Within the television category, it should be noted that the growth is due to increased spending in cable television, while network and spot have been pretty static to down.

Advertising Media Expenditures in Billions
2009 vs. 2002

Medium	2002	2009E	% Change
Television	$58	$64	+11
Radio	19	15	-21
Magazines	44	34	-23
Newspapers	15	14	-7
Internet	5	12	+140
Outdoor	5	6	+20
Direct Mail	46	56	+22
Yellow Pages	14	14	--
Other	31	34	+10
Total	**$237**	**$248**	**+5**

Source: Competitive Reporting, 2020 Estimates

Given the magnitude of ad spending, it is easy to understand why communications and media planning and buying play a such a major role in advertising agencies and client companies today. Billions of dollars are in play, and provide the basis for a rivalry between agencies.

The following discussion will provide an overview of how business is conducted by the various industry players. For the purposes in this book, these roles must be filled by your ad agency or the business owner and /or managers.

The Agency Media Department

Except for very small advertising agencies, every agency has a media department that is responsible for all media planning and media buying for the agency's clients. Large agencies may have hundreds of employees in the media department, while small agencies may have only a few people.

Agencies typically organize their media departments into groups that handle specific responsibilities. There are usually "planning groups" that develop media plans for a group of the agency's clients; if the agency's clients used broadcast media, the agency may have specialized buying groups, e.g., for network TV, spot (local market) television or radio, outdoor, newspapers, internet. A larger agency may also have a media research group that compiles and analyzes the massive amount of media research and information which is available. Some agencies also have "programming" staff who are experts in developing TV specials or getting syndicated TV shows on the air in certain markets around the country.

Media Planning & Buying Agencies

Agency media departments aren't the only ones developing and executing media plans. There are also hundreds of specialized agencies that function as giant media boutiques, providing a full range of media services to their clients who use a traditional advertising agency for overall strategic planning and creative.

Some of the media agencies—like Interpublic's Initiative Media— handle billions of dollars worth of client billings.

Businesses may also seek assistance from media freelancers who previously worked for large agencies and received good training.

Media in Advertiser Companies

Advertisers vary widely in terms of how they manage their media investments. Some large companies—like General Motors, Ford, and

Proctor & Gamble—have their own internal media experts who work with and manage their agencies or media agency. These client media specialists want to ensure that the advertiser's money is being spent optimally and that the media activities for all of the company's brands, often handled by several different agencies, are coordinated.

In companies that do not have their own team of media specialists on staff, the advertising, marketing, or brand manager provides the agency with the necessary direction and oversight.

Regardless of their internal organization for managing the media functions, an authorized manager formally approves all media expenditures before the media plan is purchased—orders placed. The agency presents the media plan to the client, who approves or change it, and ultimately signs a budget or an authorization for the agency to proceed with making the media buys.

Media Sales Representatives

Every ad or commercial or park bench you see (with an ad on it) has been sold by a media sales representative to someone responsible for buying media time and space

If you actively work toward evaluating your media and communications options, you will likely spend a lot of time talking with media reps. Like talking to car salesmen, the more you know about media and the language of media, the more effective you will be in dealing and negotiating with reps who make their livings by selling media time and space to anyone who will buy it.

All of the television and radio networks, television and radio stations, cable TV networks and cable systems, magazines, newspapers, outdoor companies, internet service providers, and thousands of others employ sales organizations that call on advertising agencies and clients to try to sell them advertising space.

In addition to their internal sales forces, many media employ an independent sales rep firm to represent them in major cities. Independent sales reps function as a salesperson working for the medium would; they prepare sales presentations and meet with potential buyers to try and sell them some advertising time or space.

What do Media People Actually Do?

The typical larger agency's media department is managed by a media director who is responsible for the quality and timeliness of all of the agency's media planning and buying.

Usually reporting to the media director is one of several media group heads, often with a title like "Associate Media Director," who has day-to-day responsibility for media planning for a certain client or group of clients. The media group head and staff works closely with the agency's account group, and often the client, answering media questions from the client, presenting media recommendations, etc. On the group head's staff are people with titles of media supervisor, senior planner, planner, and media assistant.

Also typically reporting to the media director is a senior executive responsible for all media buying. Media buying is usually done by specialists, for example, in network TV negotiations, spot (local market) TV and/or radio, magazine negotiations, newspaper buying, outdoor buying, and new media (e.g., interactive/internet).

Rather than specializing in a media type, some agencies prefer to use a local market specialist system in which the buyers are supposed to be experts on a particular market(s), e.g., Chicago, and all of the media options in that market.

Other department heads reporting to the media director include a director of media research and sometimes a planning director who provides leadership and oversight of the agency's media planning done for clients.

***

Speakers at an annual Media Post Forecast in New York recently expressed the belief that, given the explosion of new technology and new media forms, today's advertising spending waste is closer to

80%! Some of the waste is attributed to poor strategy, ineffective creative, lack of understanding of new media, and ineffective media planning and buying.

Effective media decisions involve spending the advertiser's dollars to get the maximum return on investment. Great creative (commercials and ads) delivered to the wrong people, at the wrong time, or in the wrong place—is a waste of the advertiser's budget and will not provide a good return on investment. On the other hand, a great media plan can't make weak creative better. That's why media and creative must work hand in hand. A good plan cannot overcome a bad message, but a bad media plan can overcome a good message.

In the 21st century, the changes in the media landscape will be exponential and will transform all aspects of advertising. For example, when the penetration of Personal Video Recorders (PVRs) hits 70+% in less than a decade, the audience for TV commercials will be a fraction of what it is today. As the :30 commercial dies a fairly speedy death, advertisers will be looking for effective alternatives. The challenge will be both frustrating and exhilarating. Media executives who take a leadership role in the New World order of media will be able to write their own ticket.

Chapter 2
Review

1. What is the difference between media planning and media buying?

2. What is *your* advertising budget, media objectives, strategy, and plan? What are its strengths and weaknesses?

3. What is *Caveat Emptor* and how does it apply to media planning and buying?

4. What is the difference between a medium and a media vehicle?

5. List several occasions when you may have wasted ad dollars. How could the waste have been prevented?

6. How would you describe the ideal relationship with media sales reps? Is it a mistake to believe that they will give you a special deal not available to others?

On Media Math

"Mathematics are well and good but nature keeps dragging us around by the nose. "

--Albert Einstein

Chapter 3
Understanding Media Math

"Media Planning is Both Art and Science"

Media planning and buying requires certain math skills to do the analysis necessary to make intelligent media decisions. Media planners routinely use and apply research to their analyses of marketing information, media audiences, cost comparisons, where and when to advertise, and much more.

The purpose of this Chapter 3 is to review the basic math needed for media analysis and to provide exercises for readers to master before proceeding into Chapter 4 on media concepts where one must apply the math to media planning and buying problems.

Percentages

A lot of marketing and media audience information is expressed as percentages, e.g., *The Times* newspaper covers 44.5% of the households in a particular county, or *Time Magazine* covers 20.1% of all males aged 18-34 in the USA, or a network television program, "Crime Drama," reaches 9.6% of women aged 25-54 in the Pacific Region of the USA.

Percentages vs. Decimals vs. Fractions

Percentages may also be expressed as fractions or decimals related to their universes as shown below:

	Percentage	Decimal	Fraction
Times Newspaper	44.5%	.445	45/100
Time Magazine	20.1%	.201	1/5
Crime Drama (TV)	9.6%	.096	1/10

*Rounded

Adding, Subtracting, Multiplying & Dividing

Percentages, decimals, or fractions may be mathematically manipulated in their decimal forms (it is usually simpler to convert fractions to decimals by dividing the numerator by the denominator).

Addition	Subtraction	Multiplication	Division
.15	.15	.15	.15
+.10	-.10	x.10	/.10
.25	.05	.0150	1.50

Beware of Mixing Apples & Oranges

Percentages, decimals or fractions may be added together when the base or universe is the same. They may not be added together if the bases are different. If one adds three apples and three oranges together, what is the mathematical result? Three apples and three oranges cannot be added together because they represent different universes.

In the above example, the base or universe for *The Times* newspaper is coverage of households in a particular county. The universe for *Time* magazine is men 18-34 in the USA. And the universe for "Crime Drama" is adult women, aged 25-49 in the Pacific region. The universes clearly are different—apples and oranges—because the demographics, population sizes, and geographic locations are different.

Often media planners and buyers will have to calculate percentages from a set of raw numbers. For example, if a buyer knew that there were 1,000,000 adult viewers to a television program and that 650,000 of those viewers were adult women, the buyer could calculate that 65% of the adult viewers were women. This calculation is accomplished by dividing the population subset by the universe (650,000/1,000,000).

Planners will perform similar calculations to determine the percentage of sales by market, by time of year, by medium, et

Calculating Raw Numbers from Percentages

Often the planner or buyer will need to calculate a whole number from percentages. For example, if there are 1,000,000 adult viewers and 65% of them are adult women, the buyer would calculate that 650,000 of the viewers were adult women. This calculation is performed by multiplying the percentage times the total universe(1,000,000 x .65 = 650,000).

Calculating Agency Commissions

Advertising agencies are paid for their services in a variety of ways, commission on gross billings being one of the most common. Commissions are paid by the media, although the client determines whether the agency will receive the whole commission or give part of it back to the client.

While agency commissions as a percentage of gross billings have declined over time, the traditional standard has been 15%. If an agency had $1,000,000 in billings and its commission was 15%, the agencies income was $150,000 (15% of $1,000,000).

Another common media math problem issue is to determine the total when the subset and the percentage the subset is of the whole are known. For example, if an advertising agency receives a 15% commission based on its billings and we know the dollar commission received is $10,000, we can calculate the total billings by dividing the commission dollars ($10,000) by the percentage commission in decimal form (.15). $10,000/.15 = $66,667 in billings.

Sometimes a media vehicle doesn't pay commission, so the net cost of the ad has to be "grossed up" to what the amount would be if the commission was included in the price, and the higher amount billed to the client so that the agency can receive its commission. This is done by multiplying the net amount (without commission) by 1.1765 to determine the gross amount which would include agency commission. For example, if a magazine charges $1,000 for an ad but doesn't pay the agency a commission, the agency grosses up the $1,000 by multiplying it by 1.1765 = $1,176.50 (agency commission is $176.50). Double check the math by multiplying the $1176 by 15% commission = $176 commission with $1,000 net to the magazine.

Averages

Averages are heavily used in media analyses, e.g., average audiences, average costs, etc. An average is simply a number that is typical of a larger set of numbers.

Everybody uses averages. When the U.S. Census reports the age or income of the population, the government reports the averages because it would be highly impractical and impossible to report the age or income of every individual in the population. Even if they did, how would you deal with all that data if you had it? Averages make a mountain of data manageable.

Types of Averages

There are three types of averages: the mean, the median, and the mode. The mean is a sum of all of the quantities divided by the number of quantities (1+1+2/3=1.3).

The median is the number that occupies the middle position when the numbers are arrayed in order (1-2-**3**-4-5). The mode is the number that occurs most frequently in the distribution (1-**2-2**-3-4).

The mean is used most commonly, but there may be occasions when other types of averages should be used.

Be Careful of Extreme Values

The biggest potential problem with the mean is that extreme values may skew the results so dramatically that you do not have an average that is typical of the numbers being averaged, e.g., what is the average of 1+50+50+100,000, and does the mean average of those quantities represent a true average which is typical of the distribution?

Indexing Numbers

Media planners frequently index numbers to other base numbers. This is a convenient way for the planner to quickly determine the degree to which a number is above or below some benchmark. Indexing is really nothing more than a percentage of the base number without showing the % sign or decimal. Index numbers are shown as whole numbers and the base number is always indexed at 100.

Example 1

If 30% of 18-34-year-old adults used chili sauce in the past six months and 20% of all U.S. adults used chili sauce, and we wanted to know how much more likely 18-34s were to use chili sauce, we would index the two numbers by dividing the subset (18-34 year olds – 30%) by the base (all adults – 20%).

The calculation is 30/20 = 150, meaning that the incidence of using chili sauce is 50% higher among 18-34-year-old adults than in the general adult population. One might conclude from that calculation that young adults are a high potential target market for chili sauce!

Example 2

Indexes can be benchmarked against any number in the sequence. The following example indexes each year's sales to 2000 sales:

Year	Sales	Index
2010	50,000	250
2009	40,000	200
2005	35,000	175
2000	20,000	100

The table reads: 2005 sales were 175% of 2000 sales, and 2010 sales were 250% of 2000 sales (or 2.5 times higher than 2000 sales).

Example 3

Indexes can also be developed against an average. The following the indexes actual quarterly sales to the quarterly average:

Quarter	Sales	Index
JFM	2500	76
AMJ	2250	68
JAS	3500	106
OND	5000	141
Avg.	3300	100

Table reads: Sales of 2500 units in the JFM quarter were 76% as high as the average quarter, while sales in OND were 141% of the average, i.e. 41% higher than the average quarter's sales of 3300 units. This type of analysis might be used to help schedule media weight through the year.

Misleading Index Numbers

Media planners will often scan pages of marketing or media data to quickly identify which demographics or media vehicles are most selective, i.e., have the highest vs. lowest index numbers. Index numbers can be misleading, however, when they lead to making an irrational choice. For example, if a group has an extremely high index number but represents a miniscule percentage of the target market, it may not be wise or cost effective to target the group. Conversely, a group may have a somewhat below average index, but may represent such a large percentage of the user group, that they must be targeted in order to ensure that high reach of the user group is accomplished. For example:

+ If a demographic group was five times more likely than the general population to use a particular product category but represented less than 1% of the user population, would you logically use your limited resources to target that group? On the other hand, if a particular group represented 55% of all

55

users, but had a below average index to the general population, would you target that group?

Weighting

When conducting media analyses, it is often necessary to weight or adjust the raw numbers you are working with so that the numbers more accurately represent true media/marketing values on which you will be making decisions or recommendations. This is called weighting.

The applied weights can be percentages, indices, fractions, or ratios. The weight is multiplied times the raw number in order to obtain a "weighted" number that can be compared to other weighted numbers.

Example
For example, if a magazine reaches 1,000,000 women and 1,000,000 men, but women are five times more likely than men to buy the product, simply adding the men and women audiences together does not provide a good measure of the value of that magazine's audience vs. other magazines' audiences.

So if women are five times more important than men, i.e., men are 20% as important as women in terms of buying this product, the female audience could be weighted at 100% (=1,000,000) and the male audience could be weighted at 20% (200,000), and the total weighted audience would equal 1,200,000, which could then be compared to the weighted audience delivered by other magazines, e.g.:

	Weighted Audience
Magazine A	1,200,000
Magazine B	1,050,000

When to Weight
You should consider weighting numbers whenever the actual raw numbers don't provide an accurate and realistic estimate of the value you are trying to measure. You will likely find it necessary to

- Media audiences, as in the above example
- Target audience segments
- Geographic market areas
- Seasonal periods
- Qualitative media considerations beyond audience

Excel Spread Sheets

In an agency, the media planner's best friend is often an Excel spreadsheet that the planner has created for a particular analysis. Spreadsheets frequently contain weights for the data so that a more intelligent solution can be developed. For example, in the following table, the planner examined what percentage of the client's sales occurred by market (33.3% per market). But the planner knew that the sales potential was much higher in Market A and much lower in Market C, so the planner applied sales potential weights to each market. If the advertising budget had been allocated to each market in relation to sales, each market would have received 33.3% of the budget. However, after sales potential weights were factored in, it was found that Market A should receive 57% of the budget, not 33%, and Market C should receive only 14% of the budget, not 33%.

Weighting Geography for Media Allocation

Market	Sales	% Sales		Index		Sales	% Adj.
A	1000	33.3	x	200	=	2000	57
B	1000	33.3	x	100	=	1000	29
C	1000	33 3	x	50	=	500	14
Total	3000	99.9		100		3500	100

Formulas

There are several simple formulas or equations that media planners use frequently. However, all of the equations are solved in exactly the same way.

For example, if A = B x C, then B = A/C and C = A/B. So, if B = 6 and C = 4, then A = 24 (6 x 4 = 24). Or, if A = 24 and B = 12, then C = 2 (2 = 24/12).

The most important media formulas will be introduced in the audience and cost sections, including:

- CPM = Cost/Audience x 1000
- GRPS = Reach x Frequency
- Rating = Share x HUTS

In addition, you will find yourself creating your own formulas to weight different variables and solve problems or gain insights.

***

It is impossible to make good media decisions without doing the proper homework and analysis. To do the analysis requires a certain amount of math. The purpose of Chapter 3 was to review the math skills needed for media analysis. These skills with be further applied in Chapter 4.

Chapter 3
Review & Practice

Percentages

1. Convert .35 to a percentage._____

2. Convert .40 to a fraction._____

- 10 is what percentage of 80? _____

- 1.5 is what percent of 11? _____

- 45.5% of 250 is _____

- 150% of $1,800,750 is _____

- An agency billed $9 million in media and was paid an average commission of 13.5%. What were the agency's revenues from its media billing?

  _____

- The agency above also billed $2 million net in production (no agency commission included). The agency's agreement with its clients is that the agency will receive a 15% commission on gross production billings. How much does the agency have to bill the client to receive a 15% commission on the gross?

  _____

- What were the above agency's total revenues in 2005?

  _____

  What percentage came from media? _____
  What percentage came from production? _____

10. The agency's payroll expense was 55.5% of revenues. What was the agency's total payroll?

    _____

11. 85% of a newspaper ad cost is $6500. Find the total cost of the ad.

_____

12. Calculate each region's percentage of the company's total sales.

Region	Sales	% Total Sales
Northeast	15,000	_____
Central	25,500	_____
Southeast	18,600	_____
Southwest	23,200	_____
Pacific	46,300	_____
Total U.S.	_____	_____

13. If there are 109 million households in the USA, and 13.7 million households were tuned to the TV program "Crime and Evidence," what percentage of U.S. households were tuned to "Crime and Evidence"?

_____

14. 60 is 40% of what number? _____

15. A magazine's audience includes 4.5 million men and 6 million women. The magazine also reports 2.5 African American readers. What percentage of the magazine's audience is African American?

_____

What percentage of the magazine's audience is male?

_____

16. ABC Corporation spends $7.5 million in advertising, and CBS Corporation spends $13.9 million in advertising. NBC Unlimited spends $27.3 million. What is each company's percentage of the three-company total?

ABC_____

CBS _____

NBC_____

Averages

1. The ages of some media buyers were:

Isabell	22
Sally	22
John	22
Bill	24
Kerri	27

    Mean age is _____

    Median age is_____

    Mode is _____

    In this case, which method of averaging makes the most sense?
    Why?

2. Find the mean, mode and median in the following numbers:

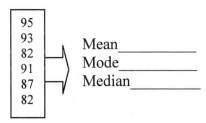

    ```
    95
    93       Mean_____
    82       Mode_____
    91       Median_____
    87
    82
    ```

3. Brand X's quarterly advertising spending is listed below. What is
    the brand's average (mean) spending per quarter?

1st Quarter	$150,000
2nd Quarter	$400,000
3rd Quarter	$500,000
4th Quarter	$750,000

How would you interpret your finding?

4. Fifteen individuals were interviewed in a research project. What was the average (mean) age, and what was the median income of the respondents?

Mean Age_____

Median Income_____

Mean Income_____

Respondent	Age	Income - $
A	42	32,600
B	36	18,400
C	42	23,500
D	43	28,000
E	32	45,000
F	37	15,900
G	42	22,700
H	44	43,500
I	40	30,500
J	35	14,900
K	41	28,000
L	38	26,800
M	39	34,000
N	40	50,000
O	42	36,500

Which type of averaging makes the most sense in this situation?

Indexing

1. Index Brand X's profit for each year to 1990 profits and then to average profits for the years shown:

Year	Profit (MM)	Index to 1990	Index to Avg. Year
2007	$42.5		
2000	35.5		
1995	34.0		
1990	36.0		
1985	25.0		

What have you learned about Brand X's profitability trends?

2. Following are the percentages of Brand X's sales for October, November, and December. For the entire year, 8.33% of sales occur in the average month. Calculate the sales indices for October, November, and December to the average month during the year:

	% Annual Sales	Index to Avg. Mo.
October	9.0	
November	12.5	
December	18.9	

What does this data tell you about this store's sales during October-December and the balance of the year?

3. If 10% of the U.S. population is of Hispanic origin and 50% of L.A.'s population is Hispanic, what is the index of Hispanic population in L.A. vs. the U.S. average? Would it make sense to analyze the Hispanic indices in all U.S. markets?

4. Store X generates 4.5% of its sales in Chicago which represents about 3.0% of the U.S. population. What is the Brand's sales development index in Chicago? Explain what the number means.

   What conclusions might you draw from this finding?

5. *Buffet Magazine* reaches 1.2% of all adults in the U.S. and 5.5% of the big eaters in the U.S. Calculate the index which shows how selective *Buffet Magazine* is in reaching big eaters. Explain what the index is measuring.

6. Using 1990 as the base year, calculate indices for Brand X's sales, advertising expenditures, and profits.

	2000	**2005**	**2008**	**2010**
Sales (MM)	$250	$300	$450	$600
Profit (MM)	12	18	35	60
Ad Spend (MM)	12	25	45	70

   Sales Index

   Profit Index

   Ad Spend Index

   What observations can you make from the analysis using indices?

7. Research shows that 16% of the adult population are heavy users of a food enhancer, but 40% of the viewers of the Food Network are heavy users. What is the heavy user index for the adult audience of the Food Network?

How would you explain <u>why</u> the Food Network has this index?

8. When can index numbers be misleading?

9. Can you think of instances where the press has reported misleading statistics based on index numbers or percentages?

10. List several ways you can use to use index numbers to analyze marketing or media data.

11. You are evaluating four business magazines. Using the index provided, weight the audience of each magazine to reflect the amount of technology editorial carried.

Magazine	Audience	Weight	Weighted Audience
A	5,500,000	60	
B	3,500,000	80	
C	5,000,000	40	
D	6,000,000	100	

12. You are comparing two media vehicles strictly on the basis of audience. Your primary target audience is males because they consume twice as much product as females. Which vehicle provides the largest un-weighted audience? The largest weighted audience?

	Vehicle A			Vehicle B		
	Male	Female	Total	Male	Female	Total
Audience	3200	4800	8000	1700	5800	7500
Weight	100%	50%	-	100%	50%	-
Adj Audience						

Purely on the basis of audience, which magazine would you buy and why?

13. A television program has an audience of 10,000,000 adults. It is estimated that approximately 60% of the audience is paying full attention. How many viewers are thought to be paying full attention? Is this a form of weighting?

14. You feel that for a particular advertising message, television is twice as effective as magazines and three times more effective than radio. First, determine the weights for each medium, then calculate the weighted audience.

Medium	Un-weighted Audience	Weight	Weighted Audience
Television	590,000 x	=	
Magazines	700,000 x	=	
Radio	1,000,000 x	=	

15. You are analyzing several geographic regions for advertising. Using the weights provided, calculate each region's weighted sales potential and share of total U.S. weighted sales potential.

Region	Sales	% US	Weight	Weighted Sales	% US
East	1000	17.5	75%		
Central	1200	21.1	80%		
South	1500	26.3	120%		
West	2000	35.1	150%		
U.S.	**5700**	**100.0**	**100%**		

Formulas

1. Given: **X = Y + Z.** If Y is 30 and Z is 60, what is X?

2. In formula #1 above, if X is 40 and Z is 20, what is the value of Y?

3. Given: **A = C x D**. If C is 8 and D is 10, what is A?

4. Given the equation in #3: If A is 60, and D is 10, what is C?

5. If it costs $10,000 to reach 1% of a target market, what would it cost to reach 65%?

6. What would it cost to reach 100% of the same target market **two times**?

7. Given: **CPM = Cost/Audience x 1000**. If the cost of an ad in a media vehicle is $10,000, and the audience is 3,000,000 persons, what is the CPM (Cost per Thousand) persons reached by the media vehicle?

8. What exactly does the CPM measure?

9. Given: **Rating = Share x HUTS.** If a show's share is 20% and HUTS are 60%, what is the TV program's rating?

10. Referring to the formula in #7, if the rating is 8 and HUTS are 60%, what is the program's share?

11. Given: **NR = A +B −AB (df),** where A is .35, B is .50, and df = 1.5.

12. If an average of 10,000 people sees an issue of a magazine, how many people could be exposed to six issues of the same magazine?

13. If one ad in *Time* magazine costs $200,000 and an ad in *Newsweek* costs $175,000, what is the total cost of three ads in *Time* and two ads in *Newsweek*?

Chapter 4
Media Concepts & Terminology

"GRPS spoken here... What exactly are GRPS anyway?"

In media, information and knowledge are power and leverage. In order to maximize the ROI from your media investments and to be able to intelligently communicate and negotiate with media reps (who are trying to sell you their latest and greatest), you absolutely have to understand the concepts and language, evaluate what is being proposed and conclude whether you should buy it and, if so, at what price.

Chapter 4 will briefly explain the most important media concepts and terminology so that you can better understand the real value of the media you are evaluating. We'll start with some terminology.

Definitions of Media

To review, media are the paid *channels of communication* that are used to deliver advertising messages to the consumer— television, radio, newspapers, magazines, internet, and so on. Media is plural, medium is singular. Television is an advertising medium. Choosing the classes of media for your media plan will usually be your first strategic media decision. After you have decided which media classes, then you have to determine which specific *media vehicles* you will use.

Media vehicles are the specific media selections you make from the different media classes as above. In television, media vehicles refer to the hundreds of programs (e.g., "CSI" or "Lost") you could buy into. In newspapers, the media vehicle could be the *Detroit News*, in magazines, *Forbes*, and on the web, Google AdWords.

In most cases, you probably won't know what specific TV programs or radio stations you will actually buy until you negotiate the buy with all of the potential sellers, i.e., everyone will have a shot at your business. Plus, if you open negotiations with alternative media, the networks or stations will have to compete with them for your business as well.

Media Audiences

Advertising is placed in media in order to reach specified audiences. Media sales people sell their audience and buyers buy audience. However, there are many different concepts of audience. The following reviews some of the important audience concepts.

Circulation

Print media such as magazines and newspapers generate audiences from the copies they print and distribute—whether paid or free. The *number of copies* printed/distributed is their circulation.

The circulation rate base is the guaranteed circulation on which a publication bases its rates. If the publication falls short of its rate base circulation, it owes the advertiser a pro rata rebate.

Consumer publications' circulation is audited by the Audit Bureau of Circulation (ABC), and business/trade publications are audited by Business Press Association (BPA). Always ask newspapers and magazines for a copy of their audit report.

For outdoor/billboards, circulation refers to the traffic passing by a location. You should ask the outdoor sales rep for a copy of the traffic audit on which they are basing their rates.

Be suspicious of media which do not have their circulation audited, providing only a sworn statement from the publisher.

What is important to understand is that *circulation* is a pre-requisite to generating an audience, but circulation is not itself audience (actual viewers, readers). Regardless, for many specialized consumer and business/trade publications, circulation data will be the extent of the "audience" data available.

Coverage

When a media sales representative calls and talks about his medium's *coverage*, be aware that the term has different meanings for different media.

In broadcast, for example, "coverage" refers to the geographic area capable of receiving a station's signals. Coverage has absolutely nothing to do with whether anyone is watching or listening! Never buy a TV or radio station purely based on its coverage. You don't want audience not a signal that may not generate any audience!

In newspapers, coverage refers to the gross percentage of households in a geographic area that gets the newspaper. So, newspaper *coverage is circulation (# copies distributed) in a defined market area divided by the number of households in the same market area.* So be aware that coverage is not a measure of actual audience or audience exposure, or readership of the newspaper. In theory, a free newspaper with a circulation of 100,000 in a market area of 100,000 homes could claim 100% coverage even though few people actually read it.

In magazines, coverage is a more meaningful audience concept because it refers to the magazine's "reach" of a particular target group For example, a magazine with 100,000 circulation and three readers per copy generates an audience of 300,000 people who picked up or looked into the average issue of the magazine. If 20 per cent of the total audience is in your target group, you would reach 60,000 members of your target audience. The number of target audience readers (60,000) as a percent of the total target universe is the "coverage" of the magazine. So in this example, if the universe of target audience people is 600,000, the magazine's "coverage" is 10% (60,000 reached/600,000 universe = 10%).

Vehicle Audience

Beyond coverage, Vehicle Audience refers to the number of target audience persons who are in the average audience of the media vehicle. For example, an average of 6,000,000 adults may read the average issue of *Time Magazine*. Or, 106 million people were watching the 2010 Super Bowl during the average time.

When a media rep comes to see you, he/she will typically be armed with a lot of data "proving" their vehicle audience superiority. Every medium can figure out how to be number one in something, and that's what they will talk about.

If they have actual audience data, it will likely be "vehicle audience" data. Vehicle audience describes the number and characteristics of people who are exposed to the media <u>vehicle</u> (not the ad). Why is this an important distinction to make?

First of all, 100 per cent of the people in the audience of any media vehicle will never see every ad. The chances of having your ad actually seen in a media vehicle depends on a lot of other factors like:

- Percentage of pages opened and time spent

- Advertising clutter

- Positioning of your ad

- How close you are to a competitive ad

- How attentive/interested the audience is

- Whether your ad is relevant to the audience

- Whether your ad is relevant to the media context, e.g., a car ad in a food magazine might be considered out of context.
  How "thick" a publication is (affects % page openings & ad exposure probability).

Average Issue Audience
In print media, vehicle audiences are typically expressed as "average issue audience."

Average Issue Audience is an estimate of the number of people (by demographic) who are in the average audience of a publication, equivalent to a magazine's coverage. In reality, the audience of a magazine, especially those that rely heavily on newsstand sales, fluctuates from issue to issue (depending on what the lead story is), week to week, and month to month.

Readership of some publications is measured, and others are unmeasured. If a credible media research company has not measured a publication's average issue audience, the advertiser has to rely on circulation figures and faith that the publication is actually read.

Several large syndicated research companies attempt to measure the number of readers in the average issue audience. Methodologies vary by researcher, but all rely on a form of reader memory that they at least picked up and looked at a particular publication.

The number of readers is usually much greater than the publication's circulation because the average copy is seen by more than one person—in the household, or at the beauty shop, on an airplane or at the library. Readers per copy can average <1 to 5 or even 10 for publications like *People*, which has high pass-along readership.

Gross Impressions
Impressions are the number of people exposed (according to media research companies) to one or more media vehicles carrying your ad.

Gross impressions are the sum of the exposures to media vehicles in your schedule. Gross impressions don't differentiate between whether the impressions are the same 1000 people exposed ten times or 10,000 different people exposed once.

Impressions can and should be calculated for your target audience so that you know how many potential ad contacts you had in each media vehicle, in comparison to other media vehicles.

Impressions are relevant when comparing the same types of media, e.g., television, radio, etc. When we cross media lines, e.g. television vs. magazine impressions, we have an apples and oranges problem because impressions mean different things in different media. TV impressions are different than magazine impressions because of differences in research methodologies used to measure their audiences, plus the physical characteristics of the media are different, e.g., television communicates via sight, sound and motion, while magazines communicate via the printed word and graphics.

For example, in magazines, we could be talking about the numbers of adults 25-54 who picked up or looked into the average issue of a magazine. But in radio, we could be talking about the number of persons who reported listening to WWWX at 10-12 AM on Wednesday by recording their listening in a diary they keep. The concept of audience and the measurement of audience is different for every medium. On the other hand, TV program tuning is measured by Nielsen's black box (audimeters) hooked up to TVs in Nielsen's sample. Outdoor audiences are simply traffic counts.

So the meaning of "impressions" also varies by medium. Different audience definitions across media and of audience communications differences make it very difficult to make quantitative comparisons of media alternatives.

Most importantly, gross impressions to media vehicles are not gross impressions to the ads in those media vehicles!

Average Ratings (AA)
In addition to gross impressions, broadcast audiences— television and radio—are also expressed as average audience "ratings."

A rating is simply the percentage of a defined universe (households, adults, children, a demographic group, etc.) that is tuned to a program or station during an average time.

The Super Bowl had a 46.4 average household rating in 2010, meaning that 46% of all U.S. TV households were tuned to the Super Bowl during the average minute of the telecast. How do we know this? Because the little black boxes (audimeters) on top of TV sets in Nielsen homes sample record what station/time each TV is tuned to.

Ratings for radio are calculated in the same way as for television. For example, a radio station with a 1.5 rating among adults 18-34 during AM drive time means that an average of 1.5% of 18-34s in the market area were listening during the average quarter hour. How do we know this? Respondents' listening was either electronically recorded (Personal People Meter) or recorded in a diary by Arbitron's recruited sample.

Total Audience Ratings (TA)
Total Audience (TA) ratings are the cumulative percentage of an universe who watched or listened to some part of the program. Audiences often tune in and out. So, the Super Bowl's 60 TA rating means that while 46% of TV households were tuned during the average minute, 60% of the total U.S. homes were tuned in at least for a while.

 That radio station mentioned above with an average rating of 1.5 among adults 18-34 in a week *cumulatively reaches 10%* of 18-34 adults during the morning drive. So, while you may not have thought that a 1.5 rating was a pretty small audience, a schedule in morning drive time has the opportunity to reach 10% of the 18-34 target.

Here is a way to graphically visualize the concept of ratings. In a universe of 10 homes (including 4 with household incomes under $30K, 3 with $30-40K, 1 with $41-50K and one over $50K), the Super Bowl reached 4 of the 10 homes on average.

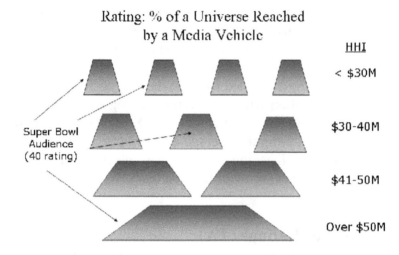

Rating: % of a Universe Reached
by a Media Vehicle

What is the game's average rating among $30-40K households? Over
$50K households?

Share of Audience

Some stations will try to sell you share points. Share is not audience
size. Don't fall for it.

Share simply defines every program's percentage of the available
viewing or listening audience (total = 100%). In the following
example, ABC and CBS are tied for the largest shares:

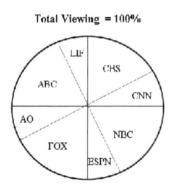

Share of Audience Example
October Average, 7-8 PM

Households Using Television (HUTS)

Television viewing levels vary by season of the year, day of the week and time of day. HUTS is the percentage of households watching TV at any given point in time. PUTS is the percentage of a group of people watching or listening at a given time.

For example, if HUTS are 30% at 12 PM, it means that 30% of the homes have their sets on at 12 PM. Another way to think about it is that HUTS or PUTS are the sum of all program ratings at a particular time.

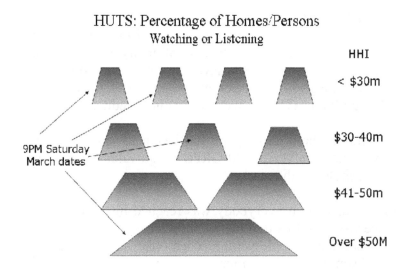

HUTS: Percentage of Homes/Persons
Watching or Listening

Rating = Share x HUTS

The formula, Rating = Share x HUTS, is used to project ratings for programming which has not yet aired. Following are the steps to follow to project future ratings.

- First, determine the historic viewing levels (HUTS) for the week/day/time of each program under consideration for buying.

- Second, considering each show's track record, competitive programs in the time period, and any changes in the network's or station's program schedule, estimate what share of the available viewing audience you believe each show will achieve.

- Third, multiply the estimated share times HUTS, which will provide estimated ratings for each show. For example, for a primetime program, you might multiply your projected share of audience for a program (e.g., 15%) times average HUTS (50%) to arrive at a rating estimate of 7.5. This means that you believe 7.5% of the households in the market area are expected to be viewing the program during the average minute or quarter hour.

Gross Rating Points (GRPS)

Rarely does someone buy just one spot and one rating. Rather, an advertiser typically buys a schedule of many programs/spots. As noted above, each spot will have an estimated household rating. Adding the ratings together for all of the spots tells us how many Gross Rating Points (GRPS) we have in our schedule.

Since each household rating point (GRP) equals reaching one per cent of the household universe, 100 GRPS is equivalent of reaching 100% of the households in the market.

But that assumes that everybody was reached just once, and the laws of chance would tell us that there is duplicated audience in the GRPS. In reality some of people were reached once, some twice, some three times, and some even more often.

GRPS = Sum of Ratings

Program	# :30s	Average HH Rating	GRPS
A	2	5.0	10.0
B	3	6.5	19.5
C	1	15.0	15.0
Total	**6**	**7.4**	**44.5**

Target Rating Points (TRPS)

As noted above, GRPS are based on households in the target geographic universe. However, households don't buy products and services, people do…people do.

Therefore, while GRPS relate to a universe of households, TRPS relate to your target audience in the geographic universe, e.g., adults 25-54 in the Chicago DMA or Cadillac owners in the Detroit DMA.

Consequently, TRPS are the preferred measure of ratings and gross media weight because people buy stuff, households don't!

Reach & Frequency

We've talked about ratings, GRPS and TRPS, and how to calculate ratings from HUTS x Share. Now it's time to talk about reach and frequency.

Reach is the net percentage of the target universe reached one or more times by a media schedule. *Frequency* is the average number of times those people are reached. TRPS will deliver some reach and some frequency as expressed in the following formula:

TRPS = Reach x Frequency

Let's say you can afford to buy 100 TRPS. Would you prefer to reach 100% of your target once? Or 50% of your target twice? Or 1/3 of your target an average of 3.3 times.

You must have an answer to the above question because it will determine how you execute your media buy.

For example, if a lot of different media vehicles are included in the buy, reach will increase at the expense of frequency. Or, if your priority is frequency, you might buy a schedule in only one or two media vehicles which focus on your target and are highly cost efficient.

The following table provides some estimates for TV reach and frequency at different TRP levels and day parts.

TV Reach & Frequency Example
Based on Equal TRPS

TRPS	100% Prime R/F	50% Prime 50% Late R/F	100% Late/Late R/F
100	58/2	60/2	38/3
200	70/3	75/3	52/4
500	83/6	88/6	55/5
1000	96/10	98/10	60/16

Table Reads: 100 TRPS in a day part mix of 50% prime time and 50% late night should reach 60% of the target an average of two times.

This is an important concept because we can also compare alternative media plans in terms of their estimated reach and frequency and select the option which best delivers what we want.

Effective Reach

Many advertisers and researchers believe that it takes many exposures of a message to achieve the desired outcome. For example, they believe that the first exposure might have little or no effect, and it takes multiple exposures to get the consumer's attention and have an effect.

Effective reach is based on the theory that message exposure *frequency* is needed to create awareness or to stimulate a purchase. There is a fairly large body of research that suggests that in the average situation, 3-5 exposures of the message are optimum. Fewer than three exposures are wasted because the threshold of effectiveness was not reached. Further, more than 3-5 ad exposures results in diminishing returns and diminishing ROI.

Note that the research is based on actual *exposure to the ads*, not just exposure to media vehicles.

A competing theory is called *Recency Planning*. With Recency, the objective is to maximize daily reach in order to reach as many people as possible who will buy today.

Internet Audiences

There are several internet audience concepts that must be understood in order to effectively use the internet for advertising.

- **Clicks** - When someone clicks on an ad or a link which takes them to your web site.
- **Visitors** - The number of people who arrive at your web site; some may have visited your site more than once.
- **Unique Visitors** - The number of *different visitors* to the site.
- **Impressions** - The number of people who are potentially exposed to your ad. However, only a very small percentage of impressions convert to clicks.
- **Conversion** - The number of visitors to a web site who take action. The action could be filling out a form to request information or make a purchase.
- **Hits** - Among web site visitors, the total number of clicks on content whether links, graphics, or text. Hits are not clicks or visitors!

Audience Measurement

Media audiences are measured continuously by a variety of research companies. You can get the data from media sales representatives whose companies subscribe to the studies. Following are the standard sources:

- **Television** – Nielsen Media Research (measures network television and local market television audiences). Network and largest markets measured with audimeters and collective demographics of panel samples.
- **Radio** – Arbitron (measures network radio and local market radio audiences primarily through diaries filled out by a continuously refreshed panel)

- **Magazines** – Mediamark (MRI and Simmons (SMRB) – Provide single-source measurement of audiences of product, service, store users, demographics, psychographics, and media vehicle exposure.

- **Internet** – Nielsen NetRatings and others measure internet ratings and cumulative audiences.

- **Newspapers** – Scarborough and The Media Audit – Both are annual large sample surveys focusing on the top 50 markets.

The preceding discussion talked about some media audience basics. Now we will turn to a discussion of media costs-- how those audiences ultimately get priced through the interaction of buyers and sellers.

Media Costs

Media costs vary by type of medium, by media vehicle, by size of audience, by time of year, by time of day, by type of creative unit and the supply and demand environment. Following are some basics:

Unit Pricing
From the seller's perspective, media are priced in time or space units, for example:

- TV - :30 basic unit of sale/other lengths possible
- Radio - :60 basic unit/:30s at 80% of :60 rate
- Print - pages, fractional pages, coloration, bleed
- Internet - Various pricing models, usually involving bidding on key words or impressions

But from the buyer's perspective, unit prices do not necessarily reflect a measure of the <u>value</u> of the time/space unit.
- Must convert unit prices to cost-efficiency measures
- Must judge impact of media schedule to determine value

In addition, it is important to remember that when buying media, everything is always negotiable.

- Pricing is negotiable
- Audience delivery guarantees are negotiable
- Where ad is positioned is negotiable
- Value added enhancements to buy are negotiable

A Commodities Market

Like the commodities market, media pricing is a function of supply and demand projected into the future. This is especially true for media with the most perishable inventory—broadcast and the internet. But it also spills over into the print media.

In general, as demand rises, as money in the market increases and supply of time and space decreases, prices will tend to rise. You see this play out every year in the network upfront market, where the biggest TV advertisers are committing billions for the next year. Supply and demand and perceptions of supply and demand can change quickly. Like the stock market or the commodities market, the media market can be extremely volatile.

Media Costs:
A Function of Supply & Demand

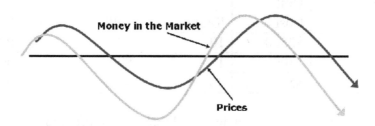

Negotiations are therefore driven by supply and demand-- as perceived by buyers and sellers at a particular point in time. Sellers try to sell for the highest possible price, and buyers try to get what they want at the lowest possible price. When they agree on the terms, there is a deal.

All of this taken together means that in 2007/2008, demand was higher early in the year. Then as economic worries escalated in mid 2008, advertisers began cutting budgets which caused prices to fall in 2009, and more in 2010. Of course, record election spending benefited television, especially local stations.

Measures of Media Efficiency

Even though all media place unit prices on their inventory, the true price is reflected in media efficiency measures like CPM or CPP or CPC.

In order to measure the relative cost efficiency of a media vehicle or a schedule, one can calculate how much audience each media vehicle "delivers" for the money. These are commonly used measures:

- Cost per Thousand (CPM) – Cost/Audience x 1000
- Cost per Point (CPP) – Cost/GRPS or TRPS
- Cost per Click (CPC/PPC) – Internet

The calculation of cost efficiency allows the buyer to select the most cost efficient vehicles. Following is an example:

Comparison of Cost Efficiency of Media Vehicles

Media Vehicle	Unit Cost	Rating	CPP	CPM
A	$2500	10	$250	$50.00
B	$3000	15	$200	$40.00
C	$5000	30	$167	$35.00

In the above example, Vehicle C is the most cost efficient of the three options. Even though the out of pocket cost is the highest, the rating is 2-3 times higher and the CPP and CPM are the lowest (Cost/Rating or Cost/Audience x 1000).

Internet Pricing Models

Pricing on the internet is different than in traditional media, so we will discuss it separately. Basically, there are three pricing models which are used for display ads and /or banners and keyword paid search. These are:

- **CPM** - Advertisers may have the option to pay on a CPM basis. This means that if you agreed to pay a CPM of $1.00, and you received 10,000 impressions (your cost would be $10.00 (CPM = Cost/Audience). Note: impressions are not exposures, most people passing by your ad don't even notice it)

- **CPC/PPC** - Most sellers like Google Adwords offer pay per click programs, meaning that if your cost per click was $.50 and you received 1000 clicks taking visitors to your web site, your cost would be $500. (Cost = CPC x # Clicks)

- **CPA** - Some internet vendors offer a Cost per Action option where you pay only if the visitors to your web site take some action, e.g., make a request for more information, make a purchase, etc

Media Impact

We buy media audiences, but what we really want is *results,* right?

Most advertising professionals who work with consumer products have historically believed that television was more effective than radio or magazines or newspapers. The evidence is where they spend their ad dollars-- with television getting the largest share.

But a retailer might believe that newspapers are most effective because they reach people when they are actually shopping. And, of course, the internet and new media are changing everything.

Nevertheless, media do differ in terms of the impact they can have on consumers. One of the ways they differ is in terms of the percentage of the "vehicle audience" actually sees a given ad. This is advertising audience.

Advertising Audience

In a sense, the first step in the communications process is to expose the target audience to the media vehicles carrying our ads. The next and more important step is to try to obtain exposure to our ads. This is called *advertising audience*.

The advertising industry has long recognized the dilemma posed by the lack of correlation between vehicle audience and advertising audience. Nielsen Media Research, the primary research company that measures network and local market television audiences, has introduced commercial ratings, which are intended to better reflect audience to the commercial rather than to the program carrying the commercial.

There are many other studies that can also help to differentiate media vehicles. For example, a major syndicated research company, Simmons/SMRB, attempts to measure "attention levels" paid to different media, the theory being that the higher the attention level, the higher the chance of getting your ad seen. Also, Starch-Hooper publishes print readership scores. And there are numerous specially commissioned studies.

Media impact has to do with how effectively a medium facilitates the communication of your advertising message with the consumer. In other words, is the vehicle audience of one medium more likely to actually be exposed to your ad because the audience is paying full attention in an engaging program environment? Or do magazines with the highest quality paper and color printing more effectively communicate the appetite appeal of your food? Does your message lend itself to letting the consumer imagine what a room full of whipped cream looks like in radio? Or are people actively seeking information for a considered purchase on the internet, e.g., conducting research on a new car? Or, is your target audience shopping the newspaper ads to find the best deal on a product/service they have already decided to buy?

We have seen that media types and individual media vehicles vary widely in terms of their audience sizes and characteristics, costs and cost efficiencies.

Just as importantly, media also vary greatly in terms of the effectiveness with which they would communicate your message, and, unfortunately, there is not one set of data which tell you each medium's impact score because all media can be used effectively in different situations. Further, there are frequently tradeoffs between audience, cost, and impact to consider

Inter-Media Comparisons

Conceptually, comparing audiences of different media types as measured is like comparing apples and oranges.

For example, consider the definition of the magazine reader who claimed to have picked up or looked at a magazine issue. By comparison, network TV viewing is defined by the number of sets tuned to a particular station/cable system on a specific day and time, combined with diary information on who was actually watching.

Apples and Oranges? Media audiences are measured in different ways for many different reasons beyond optimization of audience measurement—economics, technology, what's logistically possible, and so on. There have been controversies for decades on the proper definition of audience, what studies really measure, who is being treated unfairly, and so on.

Computer Optimization Models

For those inclined to be more sophisticated in selecting media, there are a number of computer models that can optimize media mixes in terms of reach, frequency, and effective reach. Telmar is a major supplier (see www.telmar.com).

***

In order to plan or buy media time and space or supervise others who do it, the first step is to learn the peculiar language of media. Chapter 4 introduced you to many of the basic media terms and concepts. It is important for you to gain a working knowledge of these concepts so that you can use them to help you build increased Effective Share of Voice!

Chapter 4
Review

1. What is the difference between vehicle audience and advertising audience? Why aren't they the same?

2. What is the daily and Sunday *circulation* of your local daily newspaper? What is the paper's household coverage of your market area?

3. What are the top 10 radio stations in your market during morning drive time (6-10A)? What are the average ratings for each station among adults 18-34 and adults 50+? How do you account for the differences?

4. Call a few sales managers from your local television stations. What primetime shows do each have that are in the top 10 television programs in your market? What are their household ratings? What are their ratings for the demographic closest to your target group? What are the asking prices per :30 for each? Calculate the CPP for each program.

5. If you were trying to forecast the audience for a TV program that would run in three months, how would you do it? What formula would you use to project the rating? If HUTS were estimated at

60% and you thought the show would get a 10 share, what would the program's rating be?

6. Media Vehicle A has an audience of 200,000 adults, and the cost of a page four-color is $25,000. Media Vehicle B has an audience of 150,000 adults at a page cost of $20,000. Calculate the CPMs of the two media vehicles. Which would you buy and why?

7. One TV show has a 5 rating (adults 25-54). It is estimated that 65% of the audience will actually see our commercial. What is the commercial rating?

8. If your media schedule adds up to 250 TRPS, which, according to the Reach Estimator chart, should have net reach of 66% of the target audience, how many times will the average target person be reached?

9. Why do HUTS fluctuate so much through the year and even time of day?

10. What is the difference between audience and impact? Which is more important to the buying decision and what is the difficulty with Impact

Chapter 5
Marketing Planning & Analysis
For Small Business

Smaller businesses have to make exactly the same decisions about the direction of their business as larger companies do. So, it follows that smaller businesses need a strategic marketing plan just as much as large companies do, if not more. It is axiomatic that "if you don't know where you are going, any road will get you there."

Today the world is defined by the term "information age." All businesses, whether large or small, require accurate and timely information to be successful. Regardless of size, companies needgreat marketing and advertising, the right amount of financing, equipment, materials, talent, and experience to succeed without a constant flow of the right business information.

One of the principal keys to success lies in preparing and following a good marketing plan. One can have the most tremendous product or service to offer, but without a plan in place, one may struggle for direction and waste a significant amount of time and energy as a result. Considering a marketing plan that is separate and apart from a business plan is an essential element to the success of the company.
The company's marketing objectives and strategies lay the foundation of the media plan and media buying.

The Marketing Concept and Small Business

The marketing concept is a philosophy that places the consumer at the center of the business' universe. The marketing concept makes the customer, and the satisfaction of his or her needs, the focal point of all business activities. Marketing is not only much broader than selling, it encompasses the entire business. It is the whole business seen from the point of view of the final result, that is, from the customer's point of view. Concern and responsibility for marketing must therefore permeate all areas of the business because marketing:

- Marketing strives to create customers, sales, and profit.
- Drives the whole concept of the business; if consumers want to do business with car dealers who provide better than expected service, be the dealer who beats everyone else in customer service.
- Defines how the business should be positioned to the consumer to earn
- Determines product, pricing, location, naming, merchandising, promotional strategy, sales strategy, and more.

An organization's marketing strategy as outlines the way in which the marketing mix is used to attract and satisfy the target market and achieve the organization's goals. Every marketing plan has to fit the needs and situation. Even so, there are standard components one just can't do without.

Simplified Strategic Planning

Strategic planning is fundamentally a decision-making process based on asking simple but deep questions, analyzing the range of answers, and choosing among them:

- Why are we in business?
- Where are we now?
- Where do we want to go?

- How do we get there?
- When will we get there?
- What do we want to accomplish?
- When we get there?
- What will it cost?
- What is the return on investment?

Strategic planning is a disciplined creative process for determining where you want to take your company. This process encompasses the entire spectrum of issues a company faces, ranging from the big issues of who you are, what you do, and what your corporate values are, to the smaller but equally important issues that connect the focus on the future with the work that must be performed soon to move the organization forward.

On the other hand, it also serves as a valuable management tool. As with any management tool, it is used for one purpose only: to help an organization do a better job, to focus its energy, to ensure that members of the organization are working toward the same goals, and to assess and adjust the organization's direction in response to a changing environment.

Assessment of Strengths and Weaknesses

This is the part where the small business is forced to take a good look at the business, its strengths and weaknesses vs. competition, and what can be improved. But one can't do that inside a vacuum. Industry trends have a huge impact upon how successful one's business can become. Is the target market growing or shrinking? How large is one's potential market? What portion of that market might generate the largest sales? Putting all of this down on paper will help one to sort out his overall marketing goals. A SWOT analysis is an excellent tool to get started:

SWOT Analysis

Strengths	Obstacles
Weaknesses	Threats

As the above SWOT diagram suggests, the owner or management should do an honest, factual assessment of the business.

- What are its strengths?
- What are its weaknesses?
- What are the obstacles to accomplishing its objectives?
- Are there any threats? (e.g., competition, regulation)

In short, strategic planning is a disciplined effort to produce fundamental decisions and actions that shape and guide what an organization is, what it does, and why it does it, with a focus on the future. Smart planning is the foundation of successful guerrilla activities.

The Marketing Plan

A written marketing plan usuall includes four parts: the Situation Analysis, Marketing Objectives, Marketing Strategy, and the Tactical Plan.

Situation Analysis

The situation analysis is a collection and analysis of all of the pertinent marketing data which affects your business. For example, a typical situation analysis would include data and analysis such as:

- Industry data: How big is the market, what are the trends, where is your industry headed.
- Business sales data: How big is your business, what are the trends? What are the sales of the product categories and individual products, what are the trends, what is the outlook?
- What is the future? Technology breakthroughs?
- Who are your primary competitors? What are they doing?
- Who is the consumer? How many are there, what are their demographic and psychographic characteristics? Where do they live? What are their spending habits?
- What is the consumer decision making process? How do they decide what and when to buy in your business category?
- What distribution channel issues do you face? How much of the business in each channel?
- What is your trading area? Analysis of sales by market area or zip codes?
- What is the seasonality of the business?
- What are the primary problems and opportunities facing the business? Diagnosing marketing problems usually requires determining WHY sales are trending down. On the other hand, opportunities represent things you can do to capitalize on a competitive situation, e.g., if a competitor is out of stock but you aren't, run a promotion!

Marketing Objectives

Marketing objectives define what the business wants to realistically accomplish in the short and long terms. Marketing objectives typically include:

- Sales objectives, short and long term
- Market share objectives, short and long term
- Distribution
- Market Development objectives
- Consumer Development
- Profitability objectives, short and long term

Marketing Strategies

There are two basic parts to the marketing strategy:

1. ***Definition of target markets*** - Who will the business and marketing plan be directed to? Why? Target markets in a real sense represent the source of volume. For example, if your objective is to increase sales 20%, where is that business going to come from? Senior citizens or young people?

Putting the customer first is probably the most popular phrase used by firms ranging from giant conglomerates to the corner barbershop, but the sloganizing is often just lip service. Success, however, is more likely if one dedicates his activities exclusively to solving his customer's problems. Any marketing program has a better chance of being productive if it is timed, designed and written to solve a problem for potential customers and is carried out in a way that the customer understands and trusts. Marketing is a very complex subject; it deals with all the steps between determining customer needs and supplying them at a profit.

Understanding customers is so important that large corporations spend hundreds of millions annually on market research. Although such formal research is important, a small firm can usually avoid this expense. Typically, the owner or manager of a small concern knows the customers personally. One of the greatest needs of managers of business is to understand and develop marketing programs for their products and services. Business success is based on the ability to build a growing body of satisfied customers. Modern marketing programs are built around the "marketing concept," which directs managers to focus their efforts on identifying and satisfying customer needs—at a profit.

2. ***Selection of a marketing mix*** - The marketing mix is your tool box of ways to influence your target market. It includes the 4-P's: product, price, place (distribution), and Promotion as discussed below:

+ **Product**: The product refers to the service or tangible good that satisfies the target customer's wants. Effective product strategies for a business may include concentrating on a narrow product line and developing a highly specialized product containing an unusual amount of service.

+ **Place**: The place refers to placement (usually managed by sales or OEM), such as having the product available where and when targeted customers want to buy it.

+ **Promotions**: Promotion includes advertising, PR, event marketing, online marketing, direct marketing, personal selling, channel marketing, and alliances. In general, high-quality salesmanship is a must for small businesses due to their limited ability to advertise heavily. Good *Yellow Pages* advertising is a must for small retailers. Direct mail is an effective, low-cost medium of advertising available to small businesses.

+ **Price:** Price consists of the policies regarding competitive upgrades, reseller pricing, discounts, list price, distributor, and street price (the actual selling price). Determining price levels and/or pricing policies (including credit policy) is the major factor affecting total revenue. Generally, higher prices mean lower volume and vice-versa. However, small businesses can often command higher prices due to the personalized service they can offer.

A good working marketing strategy should not be changed every year. It should not be revised until company objectives (financial, marketing, and overall company goals) have been achieved or the competitive situation has changed significantly, e.g., a new competitor comes into the category or significantly different or new products emerge from existing competitors.

The Marketing Plan
The marketing plan is the translation of the marketing strategy into an action plan with budgets. The marketing plan can lay everything out on a calendar and spreadsheets. It specifies all marketing actions to be

taken, such as a schedule of promotion, the media plan, when any new pricing takes effect, trade shows, and so on.

For small businesses operating in a volatile environment, there needs to be adequate flexibility to change course when needed. The plan is a good roadmap, but it is subject to change.

Monitoring & Measuring Results

Businesses should have a method of tracking results and providing diagnostics for continuous improvement. Low cost market research can be an invaluable tool to help the business owner understand what is affecting the business and what can be done about it.

***

In order to conduct sound guerrilla Media operations, it is imperative that there is a sound strategy in place. Good marketing information and a sound strategy provide the foundation for all marketing communications activities. The better the foundation, the more effective everything else will be and vice versa.

Chapter 5
Review

1. Why is it just as important—or even more important—for a small business to have a strategic marketing plan?

2. If you have a strategic marketing plan, 1) what are your short and long term marketing objectives and 2) what are the marketing strategies you are implementing to achieve your objectives?

3.Do a SWOT analysis for your business:

Strengths	Obstacles
Weaknesses	Threats

4. What are the strategic implications for your business?

Target Market:

Geographic:

Competitive:

Products/Services/Facilities:

Price:

Place (Distribution & Channel):

Promotion:

Other:

5. What are your sales by geographic market area? Industry sales?

6. What are your sales by month? Industry sales?

7. If your market share increased significantly, what would the source of volume be? In other words, where would the business come from—what consumer groups, what competitors?

Chapter 6
Geography:
Primary Marketing Area

Chapter 6 is about "Maximizing Sales & Profit by Optimizing the Geographic Allocation of Ad Dollars." Geographic targeting of communications represents an important opportunity for Guerrilla Media buying to save substantial dollars.

Defining the geographic scope of the business is perhaps the single most important determination because it drives everything else: budget needs, media selection, the geographic coverage of selected media, and return on investment (ROI). Geographic business potential may be defined as global, national, local market (DMA), trading area, or high opportunity zip code clusters (micro-markets).

The internet has made it possible for small businesses to compete in larger (or smaller) geographic areas than ever.

The driving principle of geography in media planning and buying is that it is most profitable to advertise to prospects who have the greatest likelihood of buying and the lowest customer acquisition cost. Most likely, your best prospects are in your Primary Market Area. In contrast, it is least profitable to advertise to those who are not in the Primary Market Area.

Paying for advertising to people with a low likelihood of purchase (because of where they live) is a waste of ad dollars that could be used to increase ESOV, market share, and profitability.

Geography and ROI

Deciding where to advertise and how much emphasis to place on which geographic areas can be one of the most important advertising and marketing decisions made. This is because market areas usually differ widely in terms of advertisers' marketing situations, problems, and opportunities.

For example, let's assume you want to target a large competitor which spends $100 million in national media. If you are located in a market the size of Cleveland, the competitor is likely spending the equivalent of $1,000,000 in Cleveland. If your primary trading area within the Cleveland market represents about 10% of he market population and 80% of your sales, this competitor is spending $100,000 against your target customers.

But, if your budget is $75,000, stretched to the equivalent of $150,000 with Guerrilla Media Buying strategies, your Share of Voice would surpass this particular Goliath by 50%!

Advertising to Unlikely Buyers Wastes Dollars!

Consider the case of the large single-unit retailer whose Primary Retail Trading Area was within a five-mile radius of the store. This area accounted for 5% of the DMA population, but 70%+ of the retailer's sales.

Based on a sales pitch from a major radio station, the retailer purchased $20,000 in radio time from the station which has a broad geographic coverage area. At least 95% of the retailer' exposure fell outside the retailer's Primary Market Area. In effect, this advertiser spent $19,000 outside of the Primary Market Area, and $1000 within the Primary Market area (5% of the total expenditure). Obviously, this
104

spending provided a negative ROI because $1000 worth of advertising would not likely generate $20,000 in gross profit necessary to pay for the advertising.

All media cover specific geographic areas, so we'll begin with some of the key geographic market definitions. Based on the situation analysis and the marketing objectives and strategy, we must identify the geographic priorities for where you want our advertising messages to be seen. Based on this, you can decide whether to use national, regional, local market, or micro market media to reach our target markets.

Geographic Market Areas

Advertisers have the option to advertise in virtually any geographic market area-- from national to zip coded micromarkets within DMAs.

National

For companies or brands with national sales and distribution, it may be decided that advertising should be purchased to provide national exposure. Network or cable television or national magazines are examples of ways an advertiser can achieve national exposure.

Which Geographic Markets?
Identify High Potential Markets Across the Country

Designated Market Areas (DMAs)

One of the most important local market definitions is the <u>Designated Market Area,</u> usually called a DMA. Nielsen Media Research periodically conducts county TV viewing studies to determine which stations the households in a county watch the most. Nielsen then puts all the counties doing the majority of their viewing to particular "home market" stations together. Every county in the U.S. is assigned to one of 210 DMAs. DMAs can include many counties because television stations cover a fairly large area.

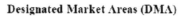

Designated Market Areas (DMA)

Most consumer goods/services marketers use DMAs as their standard market definition and organize all of their pertinent marketing data by DMA—like population statistics, industry and brand sales data, competitive data, budgets, etc.—so that they can perform important market analyses.

For example, many companies analyze their brand and competitive development (BDI) for each DMA vs. the industry/category. This allows advertisers to measure their brand performance in relation to market potential.

Metro Areas (SMSAs)

SMSAs, or metro areas, are also often used in media planning, especially for media whose coverage area is smaller than TVs. Radio stations, newspapers, out of home, etc. are usually planned by metro area. This is partly important because many large DMAs contain more than one SMSA.

Total Survey Area

The total survey area refers to the total audience of a TV or radio station within and outside the DMA or SMSA. TV audiences will spill into counties outside the DMA, and radio audiences will spill into areas outside the metro area. Most advertisers will use the TSA audience to calculate the cost efficiency of a particular media vehicle or schedule.

Retail Trading Area

Most retail businesses draw most of their customers from a finite geographic area generally defined as the *retail trading area*. Understanding the geography of your retail trading area is vital to improving your media effectiveness. Typically, a retail business realizes up to 50% - 80% of its business from consumers within a **3-5 mile radius** of the business.

Typical Trading Area

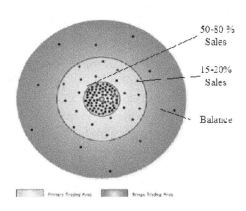

One study estimated the distribution of sales for auto dealerships demonstrates the point for auto buyers (who are willing to travel further than people do for more routine purchases).

- 55% of dealership sales occur within 5 miles

- 83% of dealership sales occur within 10 miles

- 90% of dealership sales occur within 15 miles

Clearly, dealership sales performance begins to deteriorate rapidly after about 5 miles from the dealership.

Trading Areas are Shrinking

In essence, today consumers are traveling shorter distances to purchase certain goods than previously. This means that a retailer's business is becoming more localized. A successful retailer, therefore, may increase its market share in its Primary Trading Area (inner circle), while losing share in the outer perimeters. Buyers tend to travel further for unique niche businesses with little competition or to visit large regional malls.

How to Determine *Your* Trading Area(s)

Brick and mortar retailers draw business from a finite geographic area. Customers actually define trading areas, in effect, by deciding how far they are willing to travel.

Your trading area will be influenced by several factors: your location (e.g., your trading area will be larger if in a regional mall vs. an independent location in a lower populated area), uniqueness of business, level and location of competition, the surrounding geography and topography such as mountains, rivers or railroad tracks, as well as any compelling short term reasons to visit your business (e.g., great purchase incentives and offers which make it worthwhile for a consumer to travel.)

To define your current trading area in terms of the geographic area your current customers come from you can collect their zip codes at check out or purchase. Then tabulate the number of customer sales by zip code.

To define your trading area potential, we would suggest conducting primary research with consumers in the target outlying areas.

Trading Area and Store Type

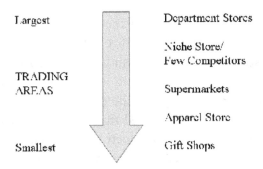

Largest — Department Stores

Niche Store/ Few Competitors

TRADING AREAS — Supermarkets

Apparel Store

Smallest — Gift Shops

To Improve Media & Marketing Efficiency...

One simple step may be all that is necessary to significantly improve a small business' media and marketing efficiency:

1) Reduce or eliminate ad spending in geographic areas with below-average sales potential and higher customer acquisition costs;

2) Re-direct those dollars to geographic areas where penetration and potential is above average

Spending Strategy for a Small Budget

1. Focus on geographic areas with above-average category sales and where your business is underperforming relative to potential.
2. Avoid spending ad dollars in geographic areas where the realistic potential for incremental sales is low.
3. Use media that most effectively target highest priority zip clusters with minimal waste.

As an example, the following is a hypothetical marketing situation in five market areas (DMAs, zip clusters, etc.):

Market 001 accounts for 35.5% of the company's sales (BDI of 229 indicates that the buy rate is 229% of the average buy rate.) The market area also is high in purchasing the category overall (20% of category sales, CDI = 129). Your task would be to decide on a business development strategy. In the example, the objective is stated as "defend" because it was believed that the company believed that it could not raise its sales rate too much higher. "Defend" would mean that the market area would receive only moderate media weight.

Budget Allocation Formula by Market Area

Mkt	% HH	% Sales	BDI	% Category	CDI	Objective
001	15.5	35.5	229	20.0	129	Defend
002	10.0	15.0	150	12.0	120	Defend
003	10.5	12.0	114	5.0	143	Growth
004	9.5	10.0	95	20.0	211	Growth
005	9.0	5.0	56	18.0	200	Growth

In contrast, market area 005 is not a currently a very good market for the company (BDI 56), but the category sells extremely well (CDI 200). Therefore, 005 could be considered a market with high growth potential with a media strategy including very heavy media weight. (Note: if the market areas are zip clusters, the company might consider buying programming on a matching cable system, newspapers, direct mail, non-traditional media, publicity, cross promotions, event/sponsorship opportunities, etc.)

High Potential Zip Clusters
You can mine the gold from high potential zip code clusters. There is a strong likelihood that there are individual zip codes or clusters of zip codes within your Primary Trading Area that offer higher potential sales and ROI potential than others. You must identify these high potential zip code cluster

Spending per Prospect Based on $50,000 Budget

Market Area	Households	Spend/HH
Total DMA	5,000,000	$.005
Trading Area	500,000	.050
Zip Clusters	50,000	.50

How to Identify High Potential Zip Code Clusters

Follow these steps to identify the zip code clusters where you can grow your business and profit:

1. List all of the zip codes in your primary trading area.
2. Compile your sales in each zip code.
3. Compile the number of households in each zip code (U.S. Census).
4. Divide sales by number of households for each zip code area.
5. Index sales per household for each zip to the sales per household for the total trading area (total area = 100 index). These calculations represent your brand development indices (BDI) by zip code. In a zip code with a BDI of 150, your sales rate is 50% higher than your trading area average.
6. Obtain category sales for your zips from the U.S. Census NAICS codes.
7. To get category sales per household for each zip, divide category sales in the zip by the number of households in the zip (as above).
8. Index category sales per household in each zip to the category sales per household for the total Primary Trading Area. This number is a measure of the sales propensity for the category in each zip. This is known as the Category Development Index (CDI).
9. You can now sort your zip codes into categories of potential as shown in the following diagram:

BDI/CDI Matrix

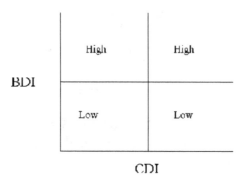

The CDI/BDI matrix provides you with a tool you can use to strategically target your spending to maximize growth and ROI. For example:

1. High BDI/High CDI – Your sales performance is above average, and industry sales performance is above average. These markets or zips are your "fat pigs," where you are capitalizing on the good market. You have to decide whether these areas still offer growth potential or whether you are maxed out. If you decide there is still good potential for growth, target an above average spend in these areas. If you decide that you just want to maintain your share of market, spend an average amount.

2. Low BDI/Low CDI – These markets or zips show below average purchasing rates for the category and for you. These are "skinny pigs"! Unless these are very large areas in sales volume, you may wish to target only a low spending rate in these areas.

3. High BDI/Low CDI – In these markets/zips, you are already outperforming the market. How much growth potential is left for you?

4. Low BDI/High CDI – These markets or zips could offer very high growth potential. Consumers are buying an above average amount of the product category, but your business development is below average. Why? Many competitors? Terrain? You are not meeting consumer needs?   If after analyzing the reasons for your underperformance, you decide that these areas have the highest growth potential of all, target the areas with saturation levels of advertising.

***

*A local business runs one page per week in the daily newspaper in a fairly large market. The full run cost per page for the advertiser is $15,000 ($780,000 annually). The newspaper has a total circulation of 350,000, of which 70,000 (20% of the total circulation) is distributed in the business' primary market area ($156,000 worth) Another way of looking at it is that about **$600,000** of this advertiser's budget was wasted because it fell outside the Primary Market Area. These dollars could have been targeted to areas of high potential!!.*

How you target your advertising and spending geographically has a profound effect on your ESOV in your primary market area as well as on your ROI.

If you have a typical primary marketing area (70+ percent of sales within a 3-5 mile radius) of your business, the further you go from the center, the lower the customer acquisition rate and the higher the cost per acquisition and the lower the profit (or higher the loss).

Chapter 6
Review

1. What is the geographic definition of your primary, secondary, tertiary trading area (zip codes or other definition) and balance of market/DMA? Draw it on a map.

2. What percentage of your total sales occurs in the primary, secondary, tertiary rings? What percentage of your total sales fall outside your trading area?

3. Compile the population, growth, demographics and category sales data for each zip code, total them up. Are there significant differences which should be addressed? (Go to www.census.gov or go to the library reference section.)

4. Conduct a BDI/CDI analysis for high potential zip clusters in your trading area. (See above for example.)

5. Research marketing communications and media that can be targeted to your trading area.

6. Is the USA a homogeneous market area? Why/not?

7. Is your home market a homogeneous market area? Why/not?
   What are the advertising implications?

On the Consumer

"The aim of marketing is to know and understand the customer so well the product or service fits him and sells itself."

--Peter Drucker, 1909-2005

Chapter 7
Who is the Target Audience?

In addition to geography, truly understanding your customers and prospective consumers is job one. Identifying, then relating your messages and media to the right target audiences is the most important marketing decision you must make because everything your business does—from selection of products & services, positioning, location, pricing—depends on how your target market definition and insights.

Set Target Audience Priorities

The first step is to select your target audience priorities. Few advertisers have only one target audience that they must reach and persuade. However, in order to maximize media effectiveness and ROI, every advertiser must first define, prioritize, and describe its target groups within the company's trading area (DMAs, zip code clusters, etc.)

Target markets should be defined in terms of size (number of people, sales contribution), purchase behavior and influence, demographics, and psychographics. Following are some important thought starter onsiderations for your decisions in defining and prioritizing your target markets:

Customers vs. Prospects

Is it more important to you to target your current customers to maintain the business or non customers to grow your customer base?

1. Current Customers - If you have a going business, your current customers are your most important asset—and your most important target audience. If you accomplish little else, you must maintain your customer base to the extent possible in order to stay in business.

The vast majority of your customers will most likely be located in your primary trading area. Hopefully these customers are in your data base with their contact information and email address, purchasing history and demographic characteristics.

The reality, however, is that most businesses experience some attrition in their customer base. Some customers discontinue buying—perhaps because they are dissatisfied with the products/services, are unhappy with customer service, their personal circumstances change, or they discover they like a competitor's offerings or location better.

Consequently, in the real world, nearly every business must generate new customers just to replace the ones lost by attrition. And even more new customers must be won if the business is to grow.

2. New Customers - Every business recognizes that in order to maintain itself and/or grow, the business must attract new customers. The question here is who to target, and if multiple targets, in what priority. The following is a way to think about it:

3.Best Prospects - Located in your Primary Trading Area, buy the types of products/services you offer, and are favorably disposed toward the specific brands and assortment offered. However, these prospects are aware of and buy from your competitors but are not aware of your business and your benefits.

4.Priority II Prospects - Located in your overall retail trading area, a larger radius than above. These prospects also are aware of and buy from your competitors and are not aware of your business.

5.Prospects outside Trading Area - Represent possible incremental sales, but cost per sale will be very high if mass media are utilized.

Consumer is King (or Queen)

Target Market = Source of Volume
Why don't competitors' customers buy from us?

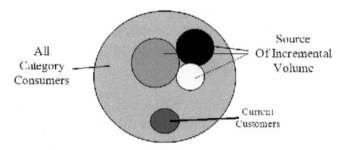

Purchasers vs. Decision Makers
In some cases you must decide whether to focus on the purchaser or the decision maker. These are not always the same people, especially in business-to-business marketing. For example, in a smaller to midsized company, the CEO may be he decision maker regarding the purchase of technology, but the purchasing department obtains bids, analyzes value, and negotiates, recommends, and concludes the purchase negotiations.

Purchase Influencers
Purchase influencers may also be a very important target group. Purchase influencers play a major, or even the primary, role in deciding what is purchased—even though they do not physically make the purchase.

Children, for example, the primary eaters of certain kinds of cereals and cookies, exert strong influence on the purchaser-parent on what to buy. That's why cookie companies like Keebler and Nabisco devote a portion of their media budgets to Saturday morning kid shows. Children exert a large influence over other purchases as well—for their apparel, foods, restaurants, etc.

The auto companies represent another good example of purchase influence. Until a few years ago, most of the car and truck advertising was directed to men, the media implication being a heavy emphasis in male-oriented sports programming. Eventually the car companies realized that while men were the primary "purchasers" at the dealership (they signed the purchase agreement), in reality, women exerted about 80% of the influence over what vehicles were to be purchased for the family.

Emerging Markets

The demographic face of the USA is changing at light speed. By 2025, Caucasians will shrink to 62% of the population as the Hispanic, Asian, and African American populations continue their growth. Baby boomers are beginning to reach critical mass, and the population continues to migrate to the Sun Belt. Of course, many individual markets already have dominant minority or older populations.

Because many of these market segments differ from the general population in terms of demographics and economics, culture and values, product preferences and motivations, it is late—but not too late—to begin learning how to more effectively target and sell these market segments.

Companies who are currently underperforming in these growth markets may see their market shares decline in the future if remedial action is not taken. Companies who feel they strategically need to target emerging markets must understand that it is a long term proposition, not accomplished with a short term promotion.

Face of America is Changing

	1990	2000	2010E	% Change
	Population (Millions)			
<5	19	20	21	+10.5
Age 55+	52	59	78	+50.0
African American	30	36	40	+33.3
Asian/Islands	7	18	23	+228.5
Hispanic Origin	22	36	48	+118.1
White				
South	85	103	115	+35.3
West	53	66	72	+35.8

Source: U.S. Census

Demographic profiling helps to paint a human picture of the target, and demographics are most used for media selection. Local market TV and radio audience data only include demographics.

1. Psychographics – Beyond demographic profiling, it is important to understand the personality and lifestyle of the target audience. Check out www.claritas.com as one source.

2. Purchase Behavior – Describing your target in terms of their purchase behavior is more direct than demographic or psychographic descriptions. Research companies like MRI, SMRB, The Media Audit, and Scarborough report on users and shoppers of different/products & services, where they shop along with their demographics and media usage. Media Audit and Scarborough provide such data for the top 50-plus markets (to subscribers).

3. Consumer Behavior - In planning media, it is also important to understand that people also often rely on different media at different stages of their decision making process, as shown below for a "considered purchase" such as a new vehicle:

Consumer Behavior
Considered Purchases

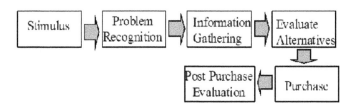

For example, for new vehicle purchasing, research has shown that seeing television commercials creates the initial awareness of a product or business. Internet search and/or seeing magazine ads or direct mail becomes more important in helping people compare and evaluate product alternatives. And, finally, when consumers begin shopping and visiting stores, they become especially attentive to newspaper ads to learn who has the best prices.

Business-to-Business Targets

Trade publications are an invaluable source of information about B2B targets and purchasing behavior in almost any industry. If you are a B2B advertiser, we suggest that you call your trade publication reps to see what they have available as well as to give you an opportunity to pick their brains.

***

There is nothing more important than understanding your target consumer: who they are, where they live, why they buy.

As emphasized in Chapter 5, understanding and focusing on the consumer is vital to marketing success, including developing media plans which reach the right people at the right time in the right place with enough "impact" to move them to action.

Chapter 7
Problems & Exercises

1. Define as precisely as possible who your target audiences are for media selection purposes. What is their purchase behavior, demographics, psychographics, and purchasing process? Where are they located? When do they buy?

   Primary Target:

   Secondary Target:

   Purchase Influencers:

2. Should you consider special marketing efforts to address emerging markets, e.g., ethnic, boomers, geographic shifting, etc.? Why/Why not?

3. Do any of your targets move through stages of decision making which would alter media selection?

Integrated Marketing Communications

Integrated Marketing Communications *is a simple concept. It ensures that all forms of* **communications** *are used appropriately, and messages are carefully linked together. ...*

-- 2020:Marketing Communications LLC

Chapter 8
Integrated Marketing Communications For Small Business

Businesses use a variety of marketing communications to promote the company, their products, and their services. Examples of marketing communications tools include:

- *Advertising,*
- *Direct marketing,*
- *Sales promotion,*
- *Telemarketing,*
- *Sponsorships and events,*
- *Public relations & publicity,*
- *Internet: email, display ads, mobile*
- *Social media*
- *Word of Mouth/Buzz*
- *Creative/Non Traditional Media*

The essential process of communication involves sending messages to potential consumers using various methods in order to create awareness and understanding of why people should purchase a specific product or service. If the method of communication is the most appropriate, then there is a possibility that the potential consumer will buy the product or service. The simple aim is to raise awareness levels, generate interest and to enhance brand development amongst consumers.

Integrated marketing communications involves utilizing the right mix of communication to accomplish your objectives. For example, maybe traditional advertising is not the most cost effective way to promote your business, in which case you would choose other tools which better address your needs.

But integrated marketing communication requires more than selecting the right forms of communication or media. It also means that the messages, themes, look and feel, and production values must be consistent, coordinated, and synergistic across all media utilized.

The following discussion will review the major forms of marketing communications, including advertising as well as other communications forms.

Advertising

Overview – Unlike forms of unpaid communication, advertising is <u>paid</u> communication over which the sponsor maintains control of content. In 2007, total advertising expenditures will surpass $300 billion in media such as television, radio, magazines, newspapers, outdoor, *Yellow Pages*, direct mail and miscellaneous. Nearly half of spending is local, although the percentage varies greatly by medium.

Advantages of Advertising – Advertising is a communications tool used to communicate messages which the advertiser believes will be beneficial either in the long or short terms.
Contrary to popular opinion, except for some direct marketing or e-commerce, advertising does not "sell" goods or services. However, advertising in combination with the reality of the business and product can help to pave the way for sales by:

+ Reminding and reinforcing purchasing behavior from existing customers

* Creating awareness of a business
* Building awareness of merchandise/service offered by a business
* Helping to improve consumer attitudes
* Help to get a business on the consumer's "shopping list"
* Help to create business' image
* Drive traffic to a business by communicating a short term incentive

Disadvantages of Advertising – Advertising as a communications tool also has disadvantages for certain advertisers, for example:

* Cost: Traditional advertising time, space and production is expensive and potentially unaffordable; some advertisers may need to consider non traditional media approaches (which can be extremely effective
* Some media have a limited ability to target audiences or geography in a way which is cost effective to the advertiser
* Planning and executing an effective advertising program effectively positioning you against the big guys requires considerable expertise
* Effective media planning and buying requires as much expertise for a small business as a large business, maybe fore since dollars cannot be wasted.

Best Practices – Some "best practices" to keep in mind when planning and implementing an advertising program include:

* Make sure your advertising plan is based on and extends your marketing strategy.
* Develop specific objectives and strategies for each target audience.
* Don't expect advertising to sell all by itself.
* Determine whether your advertising has long term (awareness, attitude, image, consideration) or short-term objectives (traffic).
* Don't expect advertising to drive traffic unless there is a compelling offer or reason to buy; the job of advertising is to effectively communicate the offer.

* Don't confuse advertising with other communications tools, like publicity.
* Don't expect advertising to offset any deficiencies in your store environment, products and services, pricing and customer service.
* Test your advertising to ensure that it is memorable, communicates the intended messages, and projects the desired image for your business.

Sales Promotion

Overview – Sales Promotion involves purchase offers and incentives to try and buy. More money is spent on sales promotion than advertising (over $300 billion consumer & trade promotion).

Sales promotion can be a powerful <u>short-term</u> marketing tool for small business. Promotion provides an added incentive for someone in the target audience to visit a store or buy a product or service.

Promotional offers may be communicated to consumers in traditional media, in store, by direct mail, or on or in packaging.

Promotional Incentives – Promotional incentives usually fall into one of four categories:

* Price incentives involving some sort of savings, e.g., a sales event, coupons, rebates, low interest rate offers, etc. In the car business, it has consistently been found that "cash is king."
* Product sampling can be an extremely effective trial device and can be executed in store, by mail, at events, etc.
* Merchandise or gifts may be given as a purchase incentive, e.g., "free airfare" with purchase.
* Other incentives such as entering a sweepstakes, contests, chance to win.

Best Practices - Some "best practices" for planning and implementing a sales promotion strategy and plan follow:

- Define the promotional objectives (trial, repurchase, frequency of purchase, increased transaction size, etc.) because the objectives will affect the selection of appropriate promotion activities, e.g.:
- Make sure promotions are measurable and you can determine incremental sales and profitability.
- Promotions should be of short duration or your business risks its image as any thing else.
- Use incentives that are most appealing to your particular target market.
- To the extent possible, utilize promotions that are consistent with your positioning and image
- Coordinate promotions with other elements of your communications: advertising to promote the promotion, free publicity, direct mail, etc.
- Don't develop an over dependence on promotion; you want consumers to think your products/services are a value at full price. (Think about how the automotive companies have made financial incentives an expectation among consumers!)

Direct Mail

Overview - Direct mail can be a very important advertising medium for small business. It is an advertising medium in which messages are sent to target customers through the mail. Newcomers to the field of direct mail often use the terms "direct mail," "direct marketing," and "mail order" interchangeably. Perhaps the best way to distinguish these three similar, yet different, terms is to remember that direct mail is simply an advertising medium, like print or broadcast media. Print media messages are delivered through the printed word, usually in newspapers or magazines, while broadcast media messages are delivered through the airwaves, on television or radio. In direct mail, advertising and other types of messages are delivered through the mail.

Direct mail is a particularly attractive option for small business owners, because it can communicate complete information about a product or service and reach almost any conceivable target group, all for a relatively low cost. Direct mail can provide the basis for a business, or it can be used to supplement a company's traditional sales efforts. For example, a small business could use direct mail to inform potential customers about its offerings, and then follow up with a phone call or a visit from a salesperson. Owners of start-up businesses may find direct mail an effective method of creating awareness and interest in a new product, while owners of existing companies may find it useful in generating new business outside of their usual customers or geographic area. Another advantage of direct mail is that it is testable, so that entrepreneurs can try out different sales messages on various audiences in order to find the most profitable market for a new product or service.

Is the Internet Killing Direct Mail? - In the late 1990s and early 2000s, some analysts predicted that the growth of Internet retailing and advertising could lead to a decline in the usefulness of direct mail.

But a study reported by Debora Toth in *Graphic Arts Monthly* predicted that direct mail expenditures would grow at an estimated rate of 6% per year from 1998 to 2008. In addition, the study predicted that direct mail's share of total advertising expenditures would remain stable at 11% during this period. "The Internet is only enhancing direct mail," printing company president Rick Powell told Toth. "Corporations still need to send a campaign based on direct mail in order to drive consumers to their Web sites. After the consumer receives a beautifully printed piece, the firm then can follow up with an e-mail message." In fact, the Internet offers some benefits to direct mail marketers, including easy access to database lists and Web sites that automate the direct-mail production process.

Advantages of Direct Mail – Some of the advantages of direct mail for small business include:

- ✦ Targeting - Historically, the most important aspect of direct mail was its ability to precisely target previous customers. If a suitable list was available, it also did a good job of targeting new prospects *in a business's Primary Trading Area.*

- Personalization - Direct mail can address the customer personally and be tailored to their needs based on previous transactions and gathered data.
- Optimization - Because of its direct accountability, direct mail can be tested to find the best list; the best offer; the best timing (and many other factors). Then the winning tests can be rolled out to a wider audience for optimal results.
- Accumulation - Responses (and non-responses) can be added to the database, allowing future mailings to be better targeted.

Disadvantages of Direct Mail – On the other hand, direct mail has some disadvantages for the small business:

- Cost - The cost per thousand will be higher than almost any other form of mass promotion (although the wastage rate may be much lower).
- Waste - Large quantities of paper are thrown away (see below).
- Alienation - Some recipients resent direct marketing being "forced" upon them and boycott companies that do so. Moreover, they may obtain prohibitory orders against companies whose direct marketing mail they find offensive.

Testing Direct Mail – Since relatively large expenditures may be involved in mailing to lists of thousands, most direct mailers take advantage of the medium's testing capabilities. Every element of direct mail—the offer, the list, and the package—can easily be tested to avoid committing major resources to unproductive mailings. In *Successful Direct Marketing Methods*, Bob Stone recommended testing in six major areas: products and services, media, propositions made, copy platforms, formats, and timing. The point is that tests should concentrate on meaningful components.

Lists, offers, and packages can all be tested in one mailing when done properly. A test matrix consisting of individual test cells is constructed. Each test cell contains a unique combination of elements being tested and makes up a portion of the overall mailing. After the entire mailing is dropped, responses from each test cell are tracked to determine the performance of the tested elements.

Best Practices - Direct mail offers marketers several advantages over other advertising media.

- It provides a high degree of measurability, for example, which in turn allows for extensive testing. Of course, for direct mail to work well, the direct marketer must be able to identify the target audience and create or rent the appropriate mailing lists to reach them.
- Direct mail also gives marketers control over the sales message and allows them to present a great deal of information about a product or service in the sales letter and brochure.
- Repeat mailings can be done to take advantage of the product's or service's potential for repeat sales as well as to sell related goods and services to the same lists.
- While direct marketing has grown over the years to employ a variety of advertising media as they became available, such as the telephone, broadcast media, and print media, it is direct mail that remains the most heavily used medium in direct marketing today.

Telemarketing

If the objective is to generate leads or immediate sales, telemarketing can be a cost effective prospecting tool for small businesses.

Telemarketing is the process of using the telephone to generate leads, make sales, or gather marketing information. Telemarketing can be a particularly valuable tool for small businesses in that it saves time and money as compared to personal selling, but offers many of the same benefits in terms of direct contact with customers. In fact, experts have estimated that closing a sale through telemarketing usually costs less than one-fifth of what it would cost to send a salesperson to make a sale in person. Though telemarketing is more expensive than direct mail, it tends to be more efficient in closing sales and thus provides a greater yield on the marketing dollar.

Telemarketing is especially useful when the customers for a small business's products or services are located in hard-to-reach places, or when many prospects must be contacted in order to find one interested in making a purchase. Although some small businesses operate exclusively by telephone, telemarketing is most often used as part of an overall marketing program to tie together advertising and personal selling efforts. For example, a company might send introductory information through the mail, then follow-up with a telemarketing call to assess the prospect's interest, and finally send a salesperson to visit.

Although telemarketing has been the center of some controversies—ranging from scams run over the phone to a number of legal issues that have been the center of debate at both the state and national levels—the industry continues to grow. In fact, the American Telemarketing Association found that spending on telemarketing activities increased from $1 billion to $60 billion between 1981 and 1991. By the mid-1990s, telemarketing accounted for more than $450 billion in annual sales, a figure that is expected to continue to rise through the foreseeable future.

Unfortunately, telemarketing has been the basis for numerous scams over the years. Federal authorities estimate that con artists using the phone bilk people out of least $1 billion annually. Some analysts contend that the figure may even be closer to $10 billion, as many embarrassed victims shy away from filing complaints. These frauds have given the telemarketing industry much bad press. The telemarketing industry considers monitoring vital to maintaining quality control and protecting consumers, so many firms ask employees to sign a release allowing such monitoring.

Sponsorships & Events

Overview - Similar to sponsoring media events like Sunday Night Football or the Academy Awards, marketers can also sponsor live event venues which attract their target audiences. The auto companies purchase sponsorships of annual auto shows as well as specialty shows where Corvettes or antique cars are on display. Sports venues and race tracks always attract a multitude of sponsors. A snack food company may sponsor an event where samples of their product can be offered to people walking by their display space. The Army participates in event sponsorships, as do builders, remodelers, and dozens of other types of companies.

Event sponsorship as a marketing tool is gaining a serious foothold in the communications toolboxes of businesses all over the world. While the concept is relatively new to the Saskatchewan market, it is really quite mature, with its roots having been planted over 20 years ago at major U.S. and European events.

Activating Event Sponsorships - Depending on a marketer's objectives and the costs of sponsorship, marketers can typically choose among many activation options, for example:

- Signage within the event venue; types of signs, how many and where they are is negotiated with the seller or rights holder.
- Product displays may be set up by manufacturers or retailers to allow consumers to interact with the product-- see, touch and feel, smell, or taste. For example, an auto manufacturer may set up nice display areas showing off a variety of their vehicles.
- Product specialists or representatives are often on hand to answer consumer questions and demonstrate product features.
- Product information should always be available for consumers to view on interactive kiosks or to take away, e.g., brochures, flyers, special offers, etc.
- Activities within the marketer's display area, such as a rock climbing wall or a product quiz.
- Entertainment such as music, magicians, have your picture taken with Batman, and the like.
- Promotional item giveaways sporting your logo-- such as hats, coffee cups, T-shirts, and a myriad of chotskies available from advertising premium suppliers.

Advantages of Event Sponsorships - Through sponsorship marketing at a community event, businesses have the opportunity to:

- Reach targeted segments of their target markets, e.g., boating enthusiasts at a boat show,
- Showcase product attributes,
- Conduct sampling and trial activities,
- Directly connect with potential and existing customers, enhancing their experience at the event, and
- Leave a lasting impression. Surveys of the general population have shown that consumers are more likely to experience good feelings about businesses that contribute to their communities and are more likely to purchase goods and services from those businesses as a result.

Disadvantages of Event Sponsorships - The disadvantages of event sponsorships include:

- Small audiences, compared to media audiences. A few hundred or a few thousand people may attend an event compared to hundreds of thousands in a mass media audience.
- Costs can be substantial in relation to the size of audience (attendees). Normally there will be a rights fee that must be paid to the event promoter. Plus, there can be significant cost involved in activating the event with a tent, literature, product set ups, on site personnel, give away items, etc.

Best Practices - As an element of an integrated marketing communications program, event sponsorship activities are most effective when they are coordinated with other marketing communications and promotional activities. For example, signage, on site sales spiels, literature and so on must reflect the same message and look and feel as the sponsors other marketing activities.

A number of methodologies have been developed to measure the effectiveness and ROI of event sponsorship. The most basic measures would include a count of the number of attendees at the event and the number of attendees who visited the marketer's display area. Some companies like General Motors have conducted test/control experiments to determine how much lift was generated among event attendees compared to non attendees.

Word of Mouth Marketing (WOMM)

Overview -- Most marketers place significant value on positive word-of-mouth, which is traditionally achieved by creating products, services and customer experiences that generate conversation or "buzz" naturally.

Word of Mouth Marketing is basically an orchestrated attempt to get people in your target audience to talk to others about your product or business. The idea is to create a viral effect where people tell people who tell people who tell people who...

WOMM uses a variety of techniques to spread the word, for example, publicity, buzz, blogs, viral, grassroots, social media, ambassador programs, consumer-generated media and more. Because of the personal nature of the communications between individuals, many believe that product information communicated in this way has an added layer of credibility. Research points to individuals being more inclined to believe WOMM than more formal forms of promotion methods; the receiver of word-of-mouth referrals tends to believe that the communicator is speaking honestly and is unlikely to have an ulterior motive (i.e. they are not receiving an incentive for their referrals).

Buzz Marketing

How do you create "buzz" about your product or business? That is, how do you get other people talk about your product or business and maybe even become an ambassador? Put your creativity in over drive!

Following is a buzz scenario used by Vespa Motor Scooters:

> "...*Frequent the right cafes around Los Angeles and you might have encountered a gang of sleek, attractive motorbike*

riders who seem genuinely interested in getting to know you over an iced latte. Compliment them on their Vespa scooters glinting in the brilliant curbside sunlight, and they'll happily pull out a pad and scribble down an address and phone number-- not theirs, but that of the local "boutique" where you can buy your own Vespa, just as (they'll confide) the rap artist Sisqó and the movie queen Sandra Bullock recently did. And that's when the truth hits you: This isn't any spontaneous encounter. Those scooter-riding models are pitch people on the Vespa payroll, and they've been hired to generate some favorable word of mouth for the recently reissued European bikes."

Welcome to Buzz. Marketers are taking to the streets, a well as cafés, nightclubs, and the Internet, in record numbers. Vespa importer Piaggio USA has its biker gang. Hebrew National is dispatching "mom squads" to grill up its hot dogs in backyard barbecues, while Hasbro Games has deputized hundreds of fourth- and fifth-graders as "secret agents" to tantalize their peers with Hasbro's new POX electronic game. Their goal: to seek out the trendsetters in each community and subtly push them into talking up their brand to their friends and admirers, orchestrating a *tsunami* of chatter for something that would that transformed a niche product into a mass phenomenon.

Another example: Rather than blitzing the airways with 30-second TV commercials for its new Focus subcompact, Ford Motor Co. recruited a handful of trendsetters in a few markets and gave them each a Focus to drive for six months. Their duties? Simply to be seen with the car and to hand out Focus-themed trinkets to anyone who expressed interest in it. "We weren't looking for celebrities. We were looking for the assistants to celebrities, party planners, disk jockeys--the people who really seemed to influence what was cool," says Julie Roehm, formerly marketing director at Chrysler.

 So how does it work? In a successful buzz campaign, each carefully cultivated recipient of the brand message becomes a powerful carrier, spreading the word to yet more carriers, much as a virus rampages through a given population.

Buzz marketing is credited with taking one online brand from 450,000 unique visitors per month to 15 million unique visitors, which led to its acquisition by a NASDAQ company.

Like other forms of viral communications, Word of Mouth and Buzz marketing have advantages and disadvantages:

Advantages of Buzz Marketing-- Some of the advantages of word of mouth and buzz marketing include:

- When word of mouth is coming from a trusted and personal source it can be more persuasive than communication in traditional media
- Low cost, compared to advertising and other forms of paid marketing communication.
- The bigger and better the idea, the more viral it may become. If an program becomes viral, the buzz can generate and engage a large and targeted audience.
- The word-of-mouth concept ripples on to peer-to-peer recommendation of the product or service. It also enables the business to generate revenue from local interest in the venture.
- High potential publicity if it captures the attention and imagination of the press.
- The internet can help take a buzz concept global.
- Potential for high ROI for successful programs executed at a very low cost.

Disadvantages of Buzz Marketing - On the other hand, word of mouth and buzz can have some disadvantages:

- A weak concept or a poorly executed concept may not generate much buzz and not become viral. The strength of the marketing depends on the transmission of enthusiasm between people, with regards to the benefits of the product being sold.
- The presence of a competitor within the generated link could also dampen the desired strain.
- If little buzz is created, little publicity will be generated.

- Hard core selling among participants (who are working for sales commissions) may alienate rather than befriend potential buyers.

Publicity

Overview - As discussed previously at the beginning of this chapter, *Advertising* is *paid* communication. The advertiser has control over the message, timing, and placement. In exchange, the advertiser pays the medium, e.g., a television or radio station or magazine or newspaper, an agreed upon sum to run his ad or commercial.

On the other hand, *Publicity* (an element of public relations), is *free (or nearly free) message placement* obtained as a result of suggesting some editorial content (e.g., an interesting story about your business) to journalists. If a journalist of editor or producer thinks your story is news worthy or of interest to their audience, they may run it for free (time or space permitting).

Billions of dollars worth of newsworthy *Free Publicity* is available for the asking-- in newspapers, magazines, television and radio stations, web sites, blogs, or most any medium disseminating news or information. Media have large amounts of time or space to fill and are always searching for good content which would be interesting or of value to their audience. For the most part, making a story suggestion to a editors or journalists will lead to:

- *No coverage* if the editor decides not to run your story-- for whatever reason. (Most publicity requests are rejected).

- *A complete story* created from scratch built around the story "angle" you suggest (e.g. a feature story on your company; a story about a trend that you present to a journalist; an interview segment, etc.)

- The *inclusion of your product, company or service in an already existing story* (e.g. the reporter is already working on a story about your field and your contact with her results in your product being included in the piece)

The Press Release -- The most important tool for making story suggestions to journalists is the ***press release***. Simply put, a press release is a "news story" that presents the most newsworthy aspects of your product, company or service in a format and language familiar to the journalist. There are many story angles, but any story must be *newsworthy and interesting* to the media audience. For example, maybe you are opening a new store or introducing a new product. Maybe you have changed your product. Maybe you have hired some new executives. Maybe you are changing your marketing direction. Maybe your sales have increased significantly. Maybe your business plan provides a good case history. But why??

The most popular structure for news stories is the ***inverted pyramid.*** In the inverted pyramid, information is arranged in the press release in descending order of importance. The most important material is placed at the beginning of the story, and less important material follows. Succeeding paragraphs explain and support the lead. Your first paragraph should tell what your news is, whom it's about, where it will be, why it's important, and when it will be held.

Your press release must also contain a great ***headline*** which will capture attention and engage target audience, beginning with the editor who is sifting through all of the available press releases. You must capture the editor's attention with the headline in order to entice him/her to read on.

Why Are Only Some News Releases Chosen? Knowing how the press chooses one news release over another will give you an advantage in getting the coverage you're looking for. Most large pressrooms get hundreds of news releases a day. When yours comes in, it competes with all the others that come in with it.

Typically, an "Assignment Editor" determines what is "news" and what isn't. This person is in charge of reviewing the incoming releases and either assigning them to editors or trashing them. Typically, an Assignment Editor will sift through press releases like you go through

your mail...over a wastebasket. If a news release doesn't catch their eye they immediately trash it. The first item on the press release that is read is the headline. If you don't have a catchy headline that grabs the editor's attention then it won't stand much of a chance making it to the next step, which is the first
paragraph.

What News Stories Get Covered -- To give your business the best chance of being covered by the local news media give them what they are looking for. Generally speaking, each of the different media is looking for specific types of news events.

- *Newspapers* want information that is interesting and informative. Newspapers like to educate their readers with timely news and articles that people will find interesting and educational. \

- *Radio* is a bit looser and has an "anything goes" type of style. Radio stations like information that is controversial, funny, or weird. One of the most popular five minutes of a local radio station here in Houston is the "Birthday Scam," in which the DJ's call up an unsuspecting person (on their birthday) and proceed to create a combative and hostile conversation full of accusations and lies. The sparks start to fly and so do the ratings.

- *Television* gets excited about anything that can provide great visuals. Sponsoring a local high school reading contest in which the principal gets dunked in a tub of Kool-Aid will get the TV station's attention.

- *All media* love human interest stories. They know that people like to know about other people. In fact, the number one topic of talk radio is relationships. If you have a good human interest story that others would find interesting you're on your

Distributing Press Releases -- To send your releases out to the media, you can either compile a list of media and contact personnel and mail or email your releases directly to them. Or, you can use a PR release distribution company (e.g., like PR Web) who will distribute your release to target industries and locations for a relatively small fee. The cost is anywhere from free to $100+ depending on the number of features you want built into your release.

To summarize, free Publicity offers small and large organizations some advantages and disadvantages-- as summarized below.

Advantages of Free Publicity -- Generating free publicity for your business has a number of fairly obvious advantages:

- First, it is free, other than any expenses you incur in hiring others to write or distribute your news releases.
- It can be argued that news stories in a reputable medium are more credible than advertising
- The release communicates what you believe is important for your business.
- Assuming that you have a publicity plan, you can issue releases throughout the year which touch on a variety of topics.

Disadvantages of Publicity -- On the other hand, free publicity has some disadvantages vs. paid communication:

- Your stories may or may not run, there is uncertainty
- Timing is controlled by the media
- The media may edit your story, for better or worse, but you lose some control over content
- If you have a timely message to get out, it is difficult to rely on free publicity as the exclusive communications channel.

Ways to Make Stories Newsworthy -- As previously mentioned, the key to getting publicity for your business is to make it *newsworthy*-- which means that you will often have to CREATE SOME NEWS. To get your creative juices flowing here are some examples of things you might do to make some news for your business.

1. **Start with your Hard News**. Are there newsworthy changes occurring in your business? Expansion? Adding new product lines? Hired a new executive? Having an antique car show? Will models be available to try on women's clothing for hapless husbands?

2. **Create Buzz**. If part of your marketing plan involves creating "buzz," use publicity as a way to help generate the buzz. For example, a Detroit area Irish bar & restaurant the held a contest on St. Patrick's Day to see who could keep singing "Danny Boy" the longest. Naturally, the bar stayed open all night. This "buzz" was spread by substantial coverage by local television stations and other media. Other than the cost of staging the event onsite, the, buzz and publicity generated was FREE and of high value in that called a lot of attention to one establishment among thousands in the market.

3. **Provide Survey Results**. Do a customer survey and include controversial questions. Write articles about the results of the survey. Media love survey results.

4. **Create Top 10 Lists**. Create a top ten list about something in your business. If you're a beautician, write an article titled, "Top Ten Most Popular Hairstyles for Women." Top ten lists are very popular, just ask David Letterman.

5. **Sponsor an Award.** Develop an annual award that you give out to someone in the community or a business in your industry. For instance, give an award to a local outstanding teacher that has gone above and beyond the call of duty. Or if you're a supplier you can give an award to the "Best" business (customer) in the industry your service.

6. **Offer Surprising Facts**. Surprise people about your industry or business. For instance, if you're a recruitment firm write an article titled, "The Average Starting Salary of An MBA Graduate is 40 percent Higher Than Their Pre-MBA Earnings."

7. **Piggyback Off a National Story**. For example, when the rumors of a recession hit one business wrote a story about how

their business actually improved as a result of the recession (It was a utility expense auditing firm).

8. **Provide Human Interest Stories**. For example, give a rags-to-riches story about yourself as a high school nobody that starts her own business and becomes successful. Remember, the media love human interest stories.

9. **Sponsor a Local Community Service Project**. For example, if you're a dry cleaner, clean the clothes for all the visitors of the local food shelter. If you're a fast food retailer, hold a free lunch day for disabled children. If you're a car repair shop, offer oil and lubes to the parents of boy scouts and donate all the proceeds to the Boy Scouts of America.

10. **Have a Memorable Event**. For example, throw a one-of-a-kind customer appreciation theme party such as a luau with Polynesian cultural dancers or a magical theme party in which customers can bring their children to watch a magician do incredible tricks.

11. **Take on the Sacred Cows** of your industry and challenge them. If you're a human resource consultant, give employee-of-the-month programs a severe drubbing. If you're a Taco Bell manager, tell consumers how "real" Mexican food actually tastes bland and boring. If you're a home-based business person, write about how corporate America is suffocating good people.

12. **Write an Informative Story** . For example, talk about the problem that your product or service solves. If you're a car detailer you could write about how oxidation and rust destroys the integrity of your car and makes it unsafe to drive. If you sell website services write about hosting problems or the effects of poor website design and how to solve it.

13. **Why Did You Start Your Business?** If you started your business because you were dissatisfied with the provider you were using (or the employer you worked for), let the press know. For instance, you went into the Italian restaurant

business because the Italian food in the local area wasn't authentic. Maybe you started pool cleaning service because of the lousy job service providers were doing on your own pool.

14. **Prove Your Superiority.** For instance, if you provide professional services, write stories on how you solved difficult problems.

15. **Be Audacious in Marketing.** Do some things in marketing which are audacious and will generate buzz and publicity. Remember when the CEO of Virgin Airlines appeared naked on a spectacular billboard in Times Square?

How you make your business newsworthy is only limited by your creativity and ingenuity. Remember, there are no boring stories, just boring approaches to interesting stories.

***

Chapter 8
Review

1. What is the role of advertising for your business? What percentage of the marketing communications budget should it receive?

2. What is the role of public relations, especially free publicity, for your business? Are you able to develop "news" which would generate press interest, appearances, etc? Can you send a press kit to the media in your market area?

3. What is the role of sales promotion for your business—incentives for short-term sales? Can you list some new ideas which might be worth testing? In your business, is there a risk that promotion could undermine your image and brand equity?

4. Are there event marketing opportunities in your primary trading area—e.g., sports, fairs & festivals, concerts, shows, etc. which could provide interaction with the consumer?

5. What is the role of direct mail? Do you have up-to-date customer lists, prospecting lists?

6. What is the role of telemarketing for your business?

7. Think of several ideas for Buzz Marketing. How would you communicate the ideas to the public.

8. Think of at least six ideas for publicity releases. Write a press release using the inverted pyramid style and a great newsworthy headline.

On Traditional Media

"Internet advertising will not replace traditional media,

it will compliment them."

--Jef I. Richards

Chapter 9
Evaluating & Selecting Traditional Media

Now that you have completed your market analysis and have defined your target audience and trading area, and media objectives, you are ready to begin selecting media!

Chapter 9 will discuss each of the major traditional media: television, radio, newspapers, magazines, and outdoor from a small business perspective The following will discuss each media form:

Media Selection Considerations

	Internet	TV	Radio	Mags	Newspaper	Outdoor	Mail
Audience							
Mass		■	■		■		
Selective	■		■	■			■
Frequency	■	■	■			■	
Geo Flex	■	■	■			■	
Cost							
Hi Invest		■			■		■
Low CPM			■			■	
Impact							
Intrusive		■					
Sensory	■	■					
Information	■			■	■		■

Television

Overview - In 2008, among all of life's activities, watching television ranked third in average daily time spent (2.6 hours per day, behind only personal care activities and work), and hours spent remain unchanged since 2003. Therefore, while total television viewing levels haven't changed, viewing has become much more fragmented due to increased viewing options. In addition, according to BIGresearch's SIMM VII survey, television ranks second in consumer perceptions of influence on purchase decisions as shown below:

1. Word of mouth
2. TV
3. Coupons
4. Newspaper inserts
5. Read article

In terms of total advertising expenditures ($66 billion measured), television also continues to be the number one advertising medium in the U.S.

	Billions
Network TV	$27
Cable Networks	16
Syndicated	4
Local/Spot	17
Local Cable	2
Total	**$66**

Television Availabilities

Television advertising may be purchased on network (ABC, CBS, FOX, NBC, etc.), network cable, or local TV stations or cable systems in almost any commercial length. Although the :30 commercial is the basic unit of sale; :60s are available at twice the :30 rate, while :10s, :15s, and :20s will usually be sold at 50-70% of the :30 rate. **Geographic Coverage Available** – network commercials will normally clear in 99% of the U.S., cable commercials will be seen on those systems carrying the purchased network, and local/ spot TV commercials will cover the DMA and beyond. If your trading area consists of targeted zip code clusters within a DMA, you will want to look into buying only the cable system(s) which target your area.

Dayparts – Television is programmed and sold by daypart: early morning, daytime, early fringe, prime access, prime time, late night, weekend, and sports. Because supply of time and advertiser demand varies so dramatically by daypart, pricing and cost efficiencies follow suit. For example, on network television, a household rating point in prime time would cost up to $25,000, but a rating point in daytime would be closer to $8,000.

Programs vs. ROS – You can buy a schedule of spots in the individual programs which most efficiently reach your target audience. The alternative is to let the station run your spots in a rotation or wherever they want (ROS = Run of Schedule). Stations like to sell ROS packages because it gives them scheduling flexibility—the ability to sell their most desirable programs to somebody else. In exchange, they reduce the price on the package so that it looks like it delivers a lot of audience—cheap. On paper, ROS might look efficient, but the advertiser gives up the ability to carefully select the right shows to target his/her audience.

Program Selection – Buyers evaluate programming in terms of whether the audience matches the target, the cost efficiency (CPM) vs. other programs, and also in terms of its potential communications effectiveness.

Program types that generate high viewer attention levels and commercial recall are those with high audience involvement (e.g., one has to follow the story). Action adventure shows in prime time usually perform extremely well in terms of viewer attention, while situation comedies or daytime talk shows have low viewer attention levels. (See if one of your magazine reps can show you the viewer attention study from SMRB).

Commercial Positioning – Where your commercial is positioned has a major effect on its effectiveness. If your spot is near a competitor or is lost in a long commercial string between programs, you will suffer low commercial exposure and recall. We recommend that you make it a condition of your order that your spot will run in the first position in the commercial pod within the program (not between programs) and will not run within 15 minutes of a competitor's spot.

Television Costs – The final cost of a television schedule is <u>negotiated</u> with the sales rep or sales manager. Ultimately, pricing will be determined by the perceived supply and demand situation. Remember that the goal of the station is to sell at the highest possible price, while your objective is to buy at the lowest price.

In addition to price, you should also negotiate commercial positioning and a significant "value added" merchandising package. This package may consist of bonus spots, billboards, turnkey promotions, or tickets to sports or entertainment venues that you could use for other promotional purposes.

Audience Information – Nielsen Media Research measures network, cable, and local market television audiences. Nielsen provides ratings, rating/share trends and limited demographics. Your rep will provide this information to you.

Audience Guarantees – Negotiate audience delivery guarantees with the stations so that if a buy doesn't deliver the "promised" audience you get money back or more spots to make up for the short fall.

Advantages of Television
Based on their budget allocations, it is assumed that large advertisers—manufacturers, retailers, even business-to-business companies—believe that television is still their most effective communications medium—in terms of raising awareness and image enhancement. As an advertising medium for small businesses, television offers many advantages, including:

> ✦ Reaches everyone but can be somewhat selective with proper program selection
> ✦ Sight, sound, and motion assist in the delivery of a more powerful message (effectiveness generally increases with number of senses the consumer uses to receive a message)

- More intrusive delivery of commercial messages
- Flexibility – geographic, timing, creative

Television's popularity has increased among smaller advertisers for two reasons, according to an agency exec who works with small to mid sized clients: production costs can be reduced, and some good deals are possible in buying time.

(Note: We strongly encourage minimizing production or media costs as much as possible. However, when you are positioning yourself as an alternative to larger companies, beware of cheap creative and cheap production if it will denigrate your image!)

Disadvantages of Television

On the other hand, television has some disadvantages that may negate its use as a practical matter:

- Cost to use television effectively (high reach and frequency) is beyond the budget capabilities of some small businesses, especially those located in large cities.
- Television primarily covers DMAs. For businesses with highly targeted zip code clusters/ trading area, local cable systems may be their only option.
- Audiences are increasingly fragmented due to the growth of cable and new media options.
- Increasingly cluttered environment and commercial zapping in households with Personal Viewing Recorders (PVRs) has caused a decline in the communications effectiveness of television.

Buying Process

How do you go about making a broadcast buy? Following are the basic steps:

1. Develop your "buying specs" based on the media plan. Specs are basically a piece of paper summarizing the key information needed by sellers: budget, target audience definitions, desired day part

mix, preferred program types, timing and scheduling, desired commercial positioning, requested value added, audience guarantees, etc.

2.　Call the stations' sales reps or sales manager and request their availabilities… which meet your specifications (specs), e.g., what preferred programming is available within your timing parameters, pricing, ratings and demographics, etc.

3.　You will receive written proposals from each station that you must evaluate and negotiate. You will determine the audience delivery and CPMs/CPPs.

4.　Let each station know where they stand competitively (e.g., "You are not competitive since your CPP of $110 is 30% higher than stations B and C"). This gives them an opportunity to improve their packages, lower their prices, change their programs, etc.

5.　Continue this back and forth negotiating process until the bottom line has been reached. Place your order on one or more stations. Don't be afraid of putting your entire budget on one good station if it makes sense!

6.　Be sure to provide feedback to the reps for stations you didn't buy. (You may need them next time.)

Radio

Overview
With over 10,000 stations in the U.S. and over a hundred stations in some large markets, there is a radio station format for nearly every taste.

Also, while 99% of adults listen to radio, when consumers were asked, radio was not ranked among the top American pastimes, like watching television. This is probably because radio is a "background" medium rather than a foreground medium and central activity.

In addition, low/non-commercial forms of radio are stealing audience from commercial radio stations. Satellite penetration has grown to 12.5% and internet radio penetration has grown to 15.6% in 2006.

In terms of advertising expenditures, radio attracted almost $20 billion in 2005 and 2006. Nearly 80 per cent of total radio spending is done by local businesses-- with only 20 per cent by national advertisers (network and spot combined). So from the perspective of advertisers at least, *radio is a medium for local businesses.*

Radio Station Formats
There are over 30 different radio formats in the U.S., although stations sometimes switch formats to try to ride trends and garner a larger share of an audience which can increase the price of their spots. The top 10 formats include:

	# Stations
Country	2019
News/Talk	1324
Oldies	773
Hispanic	703
Adult Contemporary	884
Top 40	502
Sports	497
Classic Rock	461
Adult Standards	405
Hot AC	380

Radio Availabilities – Radio advertising may be purchased on networks or local stations. While various commercial lengths may be purchased, the :60 commercial is the basic unit of sale, and many stations try to charge 80 per cent of the minute rate for a :30 (stations dislike :30s because they create even more commercial clutter).

Radio Audiences – Because there are so many radio stations and there are relatively few listeners at a given time, radio audiences/ratings are very small. A very high rated spot in a market may be less than a 1.0

rating. Therefore, in order to generate acceptable reach and frequency in radio will probably schedules on several stations as one station's cumulative audience may be less than 10% of the target audience.

Geographic Coverage – Network radio commercial clearances will likely not be fully national (i.e., clearing in every market) as station clearances vary considerably by network. If you are interested in network radio, study the station list and clearances in the markets you are most interested in.

Most radio stations have much smaller geographic coverage areas than television. The rule of thumb would be that radio stations cover the metropolitan area (SMSA), but most won't effectively cover large DMAs because their signals don't go as far out.

If your trading area is smaller than the DMA, radio will more tightly target it with less "waste."

Dayparts – Radio spots are normally sold by dayparts, with the largest available audiences in morning and afternoon drive times.

	Time
Morning Drive	6-10A
Day	10A-3P
Afternoon Drive	3-7P
Night	After 7P

While stations like to sell spots based on an average audience for the whole daypart, obviously, audiences will vary by hour. You should study audience flow to help you *negotiate a schedule that delivers an above average audience.*

Like TV stations, radio stations also like to sell ROS schedules that allow the station to slot in your spots where they want. ROS gives stations more scheduling flexibility, and allows them to save their best availabilities for favored advertisers. Buying ROS is probably not to your advantage. Instead, try to lock in specific times where the station's audience is the largest.

Commercial Positioning – Where your radio commercial is positioned in a station's commercial string has a huge effect on the commercial's effectiveness (heard/recalled). Many stations run so many commercials in a pod that you will get lost in the clutter and communicate very little of your message to very few people in the supposed audience. Also, do not allow stations to run your spot near competitive spots (require at least 15 minute separation), as this will diminish your commercial recall as well.

Radio Costs – Also, as with television, the final cost of a radio schedule is <u>negotiated</u> with the station's sales rep or sales manager. Ultimately, pricing will be determined by the perceived supply and demand situation. Remember that the goal of the station is to sell at the highest possible price, while your objective is to buy at the lowest price.

Radio Merchandising Package - In addition to price, you should also negotiate commercial positioning and a significant "value added" merchandising package. This is an area where radio stations excel over television stations. Many stations even employ a promotion manager to work with advertisers

The merchandising package may consist of a turnkey promotion, promoted on air, remote broadcasts at the advertiser's place of business, bonus spots, billboards, turnkey promotions, tickets to sports or entertainment venues (which you could use for other promotional purposes), etc.

Audience Information – Using a panel of diary keepers, Arbitron measures network and local market radio audiences. Arbitron provides ratings, shares, and "listeners" by station and time period, trends and limited demographics. **Your rep must provide this information to you.**

Audience Guarantees – Although it is usually impossible to conduct an accurate post buy analysis of a radio schedule, because in many markets are surveyed only twice a year you should nonetheless negotiate audience guarantees based on the next ratings report.

Advantages of Radio

Radio offers a number of potential advantages for small businesses

- Radio formats can more tightly target certain demographics and lifestyles—from teens to older adults
- The cost of radio (CPP) is usually less than 50% of the CPP for television
- Less wasted audience/cost for advertisers who have a trading area inside the DMA and metro area
- More affordable for some smaller advertisers
- Creatively, radio can offer great "theatre of the mind"
- Opinion: Because the majority of radio commercials are not very intrusive and involving, the big challenge is for advertisers to create intrusive, relevant breakthrough creative for radio

Disadvantages of Radio

On the other hand, radio has some disadvantages, particularly in the area of communications effectiveness:

- Because radio is a background medium and is cluttered with many commercials per pod, the audience usually is not paying full attention, which makes it more difficult to get commercials exposed and heard. (Note: News and talk formats garner higher attention levels than music formats.)
- If visual images—like logos, packaging, and food—need to be communicated, radio has no pictures (duh!).
- It is difficult to create great creative because of radio's lack of intrusiveness and obvious communications limitations.

Buying Process – Similar to TV

Radio buys are made similarly to television buys as described below:

1.   Develop your "buying specs," including budgets, target audience definitions, dayparts, preferred times, timing, desired commercial positioning, desired value added, audience guarantees, etc.

2.   Develop reach and frequency objectives for your buy. These objectives will affect how many stations you need to buy. (Individual stations may not reach enough different people in the market area), so you will probably need several stations.

3.   Call the stations' sales reps or sales manager and request their avails based on your specs.

4.   You will receive proposals from each station that must be evaluated and negotiated.

5.   Let each station know where they stand competitively so that they can improve their packages, lower their prices, etc.

6.   Continue the negotiating process until the bottom line has been reached.

7.   Conduct a reach and frequency analysis on the best schedule possibilities, different station mixes, and budget allocations.

8.   Place your order on the selected stations.

Be sure to provide feedback to the reps for stations you didn't buy (you may need them later).

Newspapers

Overview
As newspaper circulation continues its long-term spiral downward, part of the reader and ad revenue gap has been picked up by newspapers' web editions. Nielsen reported that in 2006, 63% of

adults were reached yesterday by a newspaper, while Scarborough reported 55%.

Newspaper ad revenues were up marginally in 2006, reaching $49 billion, of which $41 billion was from local advertisers.

Newspaper Availabilities
National, local daily, suburban, lifestyle, ethnic, and college newspapers offer a wide array of advertising availabilities. Ads may be of any size and shape in black and white or color (quality of color reproduction has improved greatly in recent years), including:

* Run of Paper (ROP) advertising - where the newspaper decides where your ad runs in the paper (you can request position)
* Or the ad may be ordered to run in a particular section, e.g., sports, business, etc.
* Sunday supplements
* Free standing inserts
* Polybags & sampling
* Newspaper websites
* Comics
* Classified & display classified

Geographic Editions Available – Daily newspapers offer full-run editions throughout their coverage area or zoned editions (usually on certain days) which target specific geographic areas within the market.

In addition, freestanding inserts in newspapers can be targeted to specified zip codes. Suburban or community newspapers, of course, cover their particular communities.

Sections – Ads may run in any section of the paper. Following are average weekday readership percentages for men and women:

	News	Business	Sports	Entertain
Men	89%	67%	76%	57%
Women	91%	56%	48%	53%

Source: NAA

Ad Positioning – Where your ad is positioned within the newspaper is important. Page three in main news is probably the best position in the paper because virtually every reader will turn to it. There does not seem to be a readership advantage to be positioned in a particular section unless there is a tie in of content.

Newspaper Costs – Newspapers are the only advertising medium in America that still charge national advertisers a significantly higher rate than local advertisers. (Note the small percentage of their sales coming from national advertisers.)

Advertising Rate Card - A rate card is a document provided by a newspaper or other print publication featuring the organization's rates for advertising. It may also detail any deadlines, demographics, policies, additional fees and artwork requirements. The smaller the publication, the less information that may be available in the rate card.

Some larger newspapers may have complex rate cards detailing all of their various discount programs. Some even have a rate card for a particular category of advertising. They will have their rates broken down by retail display, classified, display classified, business, even higher national ad rates.

Rate cards help the retailer understand what types of ad sizes, discounts and other advertising the publication has to offer. When choosing a newspaper or print media, you can use rate cards to compare ad rates based on circulation before you buy advertising space. Many newspapers post their rates online at their website.

Calculating Display Ad Rates -When calculating the rates for a display ad, determine the number of column inches in an ad. Multiply the number of columns wide by the number of inches deep. For example, a 3 columns by 2 inch ad is 6 total column inches. If the newspaper's columns measure 1 3/8", then we can assume this ad is 3 3/8" wide by 2" deep. If the open rate (without any discounts) is $8.00 per column inch, six column inches x $8.00 per inch equals a total of $48 for the ad.

Display Advertising Mechanical Measurements - There may be some variation in measuring ad space in different publications. Here are the definitions of column inch, standard advertising unit and pica:

Column inch: Display advertising's primary space measurement. This is generally one column wide by one inch deep. It may vary by publication.

Standard Advertising Unit (SAU): Ad size formats that may be accepted in different daily newspapers. This standard was created to make it easier for a large advertiser to place the same ad in many different newspapers without adjusting the ad to different column specifications.

Newspaper Audience Information – Two research companies provide local market audience data: Scarborough and The Media Audit. In addition, many newspapers conduct their own studies of audience, research, and effectiveness. Your rep should provide this information to you.

Circulation Guarantees – Newspapers base their rates on a defined level of circulation (rate base). If a newspaper falls below its rate base, it owes you a credit or make-goods to proportionately offset your loss of circulation (e.g., an 8% shortfall in rate base circulation = an 8% price reduction.

Advantages of Newspapers
Newspapers offer important advantages for local retailers whose target audience is current shoppers:

- Editorial/news context provides a sense of immediacy and "buy now."
- Newspapers reach 50-60+ percent of adults daily, with a higher reach of older, upper income adults.
- When people have decided to buy something—furniture, car, apparel, etc., they search the newspaper ads for price comparisons among retailers.

* Some papers can target local trading areas through zoned editions or inserts dropped in certain zip code clusters.

Disadvantages of Newspapers

On the other hand, newspapers have some disadvantages that the advertiser must weigh against the advantages:

* Newspapers are extremely expensive, both from the standpoint of out-of-pocket cost for a large ad and the high CPM premium paid for the ad. For example, a half page in the Sunday *New York Times* would cost a national advertiser almost $70,000 for 650,000 circulation, which is a CPM of over $100. Is it worth it?

* Ad clutter is extremely high, and combined with ad stacking, this makes it extremely difficult (especially for smaller ads) to stand out, be seen, and be read.

* Audiences are increasingly fragmented due to the growth of cable and new media options.

* Increasingly cluttered environment has caused a decline in the effectiveness of television

* While production values and color have generally improved, it varies by paper.

* Logistically, the lack of uniformity in newspaper sizes, layouts, color capabilities, and advertising rates make the medium more complex to use.

Buying Process

Following are the basics in purchasing newspaper ads:

1. Before placing an insertion order for an ad, be sure you understand the terms and conditions of advertising with the newspaper. In many cases where there may be a conflict between the insertion order and the rate card, the rate card will be the deciding factor.

2. This does not mean the prices on the rate card are fixed. Most retailers will find the paper's sales rep will offer special rates for first-time advertisers or other discounts. If

you're interested in advertising within a particular publication, check its website or call the office and ask for a copy of their current rate card. Many newspapers and magazines have their rate cards available online in a PDF format.

3. Newspaper rates have become increasingly negotiable for off rate card deals. Newspaper ad revenues are and will continue to be soft.

4. Try to negotiate a significantly better price! Understand that negotiations are a two-way street and you will stand a better chance of getting price and other concessions if you are able to offer the newspaper something it wants—like a commitment for an increased volume of business. Example: General Motors negotiated off-card deals with newspapers based on guarantees of certain ad volumes.

Magazines

Overview
There are approximately 17,000 magazines in the U.S. serving almost every consumer and business interest and need, including magazines in the business, home, travel, and other categories distributed exclusively in local markets.

In 2006, advertisers spent about $19 billion in magazines, up almost 25% vs. 2002. According to a study conducted by Nielsen Media Research for the TVB, magazines reach about 51% of adults on a daily basis.

Magazine Availabilities
Magazines target almost every conceivable demographic and lifestyle/interest category for both consumer and business markets. *Standard Rate and Data (SRDS)*, likely available in your library, classifies magazines by subject matter and detailed information on each magazines' editorial content, circulation and rates. (Note: there are separate editions of SRDS for consumer magazines and business & trade publications.)

While magazines prefer to sell ads on a run-of-book basis (they decide where in the magazine to put your ad), you can often negotiate special positioning, e.g., on a cover, page one, or within some relevant editorial content related to your business.

Magazines also offer special space units—inserts printed special paper, micro-encapsulation (smell the coffee), advertorials (which are sponsored advertising sections on a particular editorial subject, e.g., for a price, a computer company could sponsor a special section a, written by the magazine about computers).

Geographic Editions Available – Contrary to the perception that magazines are only for national advertisers, there are many ways for regional and local advertisers to use magazines.

Local Magazines. Many cities have local lifestyle, food, entertainment, travel, ethnic, and/or business magazines. These magazines target different audiences with circulation concentrated in individual local market areas. If your market area effectively covers the DMA, local magazines could be a possibility for you.

Local Editions of National Magazines. Most of the larger national magazines offer regional and local market editions. For example, you could buy a full-page ad in *Time* or *Newsweek* that would appear only in the region or market(s) you ordered. The circulation mailed to subscribers in Buffalo would contain your ad, but not the copies mailed to Indianapolis. Of course, magazines charge a cost efficiency (CPM) premium for the targeting.

Media Networks (MNI). In addition to targeting ads to local markets in individual magazines, you can order ads in a group of magazines targeted to various audiences on a market-by-market basis. Media Networks (MNI)—owned by Time Warner) offers networks of magazines targeted to specific types of consumers within local markets. For example, some of MNI's networks include:

- News – *Time, Newsweek, U.S. News, Sports Illustrated*
- Executive – *Business Week, Forbes, Fortune, Inc.*, etc.
- Hispanic – *Latina, People Hispanic*, others
- Home – *House Beautiful, Cooking Light*, others
- Luxury – *Food & Wine, In Style*, others
- Lifestyle – *Golf, Golf Digest, Esquire*
- Family – *Parenting, Parents, Family Fun*

Magazine Costs

Like newspapers, magazines publish rate cards detailing their rates and discount structures for different ad sizes, colorations, any special editorial editions, and geographic editions. Magazine rate cards also usually include basic circulation data, closing dates for when they need ad materials for a particular issue, as well as the mechanical specifications for an ad (page size, etc.).

Magazines like to stay on their rate cards, so the advertiser will need to have some creative negotiating tactics to obtain rate or other concessions from magazines. We discuss some magazine negotiating tips below.

Magazine Audience Information – The two primary sources of magazine audience information are Media Mark Research (MRI) and Simmons Market Research Bureau (SMRB). Both studies are large sample (25,000+) annual surveys of consumers that provide single-source data on consumer behavior in hundreds of market segments, their demographics, and which media they are exposed to. Want to know how many people bought a Toyota Camry? Their demographics and psychographics? Whether they read *People* magazine?

In addition, some magazines will commission their own readership studies—if they are not measured by MRI or SMRB—or if they don't like the results!

Your magazine rep will provide you with this data for all of the competitive magazines in the category. If you have additional questions, ask them to do a special analysis or some cross tabs for you.

Circulation Guarantees – Like newspapers, the vast majority of magazines have a circulation rate base—the circulation they guarantee at a given page rate. If they guarantee 1,000,000 circulation but deliver only 500,000, they owe you a 50% rebate. Check their circulation audit statements from ABC or BPA. Be leery of publications which are not audited and provide only "sworn publisher statements."

Magazine Ad Recall by Type of Ad – The average recall of ads in magazines varies by size, coloration, and positioning of the ad within the magazine. The following table shows the average ad recall vs. cost indices by type of position compared to the average page (index = 100):

	Recall Index	Cost Index
Full Page	100	100
Inside Front Cover	112	100
3rd Cover	100	100
Back Cover	115	120+
Multi Page Unit	117	400
Spread	112	200
Fractional Page	81	40

When related to cost, assuming you can negotiate no cost premium for the second cover, you should receive at least a 12% bonus in ad recall. Multi-page units are not efficient for ad recall (although still may be worth the premium if you have a complex story). Spreads (two pages) are not efficient for recall, while fractional pages are.

Advantages of Magazines

Magazines can offer *certain* small businesses with some interesting benefits:

◆ There are magazines that target almost every conceivable consumer or business market/audience—from auto or wine enthusiasts to highly specialized trade audiences.

* A relevant editorial context can enhance interest in your related ad
* Good for couponing and promotional offers
* The right magazines could help improve your image, credibility, and stature, especially if undiscovered by your competitors "own"
* If your competitors are not using magazines, they could provide you with a niche
* As part of a media mix, e.g., used in combination with television and the internet, research has found that magazines can provide incremental effectiveness.

Disadvantages of Magazines

On the other hand, magazines have some disadvantages for small business:

* Selective perception – Readers can easily skip over ads that are not of interest to them or that cause discomfort.
* If your message requires immediacy, magazines may not be a good fit. Magazines accumulate their audiences slowly over time (monthly magazine audience takes months to reach 100%), and they can have long lead times for when they need your ad.
* Small magazines are frequently not cost efficient.
* Even though magazines do offer some geographic flexibility, it may be insufficient to cover your primary trading area.

Buying Process

The process for buying ads in magazines is similar to that described for newspapers.

1. Contract: Be sure you understand the terms and conditions of advertising with the magazine, especially as it relates to the amount of advertising you must run in order to obtain the contract rate. If you fall short of meeting your volume commitment, you will be short rated on your previous ads within the contract year.

This does not mean the prices on the rate card are fixed. Most retailers will find the paper's sales rep will offer special rates for first time advertisers or other discounts. If you're interested in advertising within a particular publication, check their website or call the office and ask for a copy of their current rate card. Many newspapers and magazines have their rate cards available online in a PDF format.

2. Issue an insertion order to the magazine along with creative/production materials for each ad. Magazine ad rates have become increasingly negotiable for off rate card deals. Newspaper ad revenues are and will continue to be soft. Try to negotiate a significantly better price! Understand that negotiations are a two way street, and you will stand a better chance of getting price and other concessions if you are able to offer the newspaper something it wants—like a certain volume of business. Example: General Motors negotiated off-card deals with magazines based on guarantees of certain ad volumes.

Out of Home

Overview
Out-of-home (outdoor) advertising expenditures have been relatively stable at about $6 billion for the past few years. Of that, nearly 60% is local advertising/40% national advertising. About 96% of adults will pass by outdoor locations during the average week.

Availabilities
There are around 500,000 outdoor locations availle, including many different kinds of outdoor units:

* *Billboards* – 30 sheet posters, 8 sheet posters, permanent bulletins, and spectacular and electronic units
* *Street Furniture*: benches, shelters, phone booths, etc.
* *Transit*: Bus, train, transit, airport

+ *Alternative*: outdoor & furniture wraps, wrapped cars, inside buses & trains, etc.

Audience Measurement

The Traffic Audit Bureau for Media Measurement Inc. (TAB) was established in 1933 as a non-profit organization whose historical mission has been to audit the circulation of out-of-home media in the United States. Recently TAB's role has been expanded to lead and/or support other major out of home industry research initiatives. Governed by a tripartite board comprised of advertisers, agencies, and media companies, the TAB acts an independent auditor for traffic circulation in accordance to guidelines established by its Board of Directors. Similarly, in Canada, the Canadian Outdoor Measurement Bureau (COMB) was formed in 1965 as a non-profit organization independently operated by representatives comprised of advertisers, advertising agencies, and members of the Canadian out-of-home advertising industry. COMB is charged with the verification of traffic circulation for the benefit of the industry and its users (Chen 1999).

Advantages of Outdoor

While it is obviously difficult to lump all of the kinds of outdoor together for an assessment, the following advantages for small businesses are general:

+ High reach and frequency potential; 96% of adults pass buy outdoor locations every week.
+ If your business would benefit from directionals for travelers, outdoor fills the bill.
+ Outdoor can help build awareness of something very simple: a name, an image, a graphic, or a very short slogan of copy.
+ Outdoor provides a lot of geographic flexibility. Thirty sheet and 8 sheet posters, for example, can be placed in targeted zip cods and neighborhoods.
+ In most cases, outdoor is supplemental and complementary to other media activities, not the primary medium.

Disadvantages of Outdoor

On the other hand, outdoor has some disadvantages for small businesses:

- Can effectively communicate only a short, simple message.
- Audiences are mostly unmeasured; traffic counts are not a good measurement of audience as the passersby may not even notice the outdoor boards.
- Availabilities are lowest in upscale areas.
- Location of boards behind obstructions or far away requires that someone physically "ride the boards" to make sure they are well located and visible.
- The low CPMs touted by reps are really not low if communication effectiveness is taken into account.

Buying Process

The process for buying outdoor includes the following:

- Call the outdoor companies or reps selling outdoor in your market area, e.g., Lamar, 3M, Gannett, etc.
- Give the reps your buying specs (like a broadcast buy); sometimes there will be competing outdoor companies, sometimes one company will own the market.
- Study the market's supply & demand situation, how much outdoor is available, etc.
- Evaluate their submissions in terms of audience delivery and CPMs.
- Negotiate a better deal using the leverage that you may spend the money in other media.

***

There are always three basic and equally important considerations in selecting media: Size and quality of audience, communications impact of ads in the medium and the cost of the ads.

This information must be weighed simultaneously in order to arrive at the most cost effective media selection decisions. All media have strengths and weaknesses for different tasks, and the planner has to determine which best meet the needs of a particular situation.

Chapter 9
Problems & Exercises

1. What is your media mix (% in television, radio, etc.)? <u>Why</u> do you use each medium?

2. If you were to utilize television, what would you do—e.g., geographic, programming types, CPMs, etc., to maximize cost effectiveness?

3. If you were to utilize radio, what would you do—e.g., geographic, pro2.? If you were to utilize television, what would you do—e.g., geographic, programming types, CPMs, etc. to maximize cost effectiveness?

4. If you were to utilize magazines, what would you do—e.g., geographic, programming types, CPMs, etc. to maximize cost effectiveness?

Chapter 10
Internet Strategies for Small Business

An effective presence on the internet is absolutely essential to the success of every small business in the 21st century. The right website, properly promoted (to generate traffic), can help level the playing field with larger businesses. Your web presence can even give you a <u>competitive edge</u>. A highly professional, but low cost website will:

- *Provide information about your company, products & services to people who are seeking that information <u>when</u> they are seeking it*
- *Give your business credibility regardless of your physical brick & mortar facilities*
- *Give you the ability to compete locally, nationally and globally*
- *Allow you to take orders and leads 24/7*
- *Assist with customer services and support24/7*
- *Save employee time and expense by making operations more efficient*

Chapter 10 focuses on the importance of building a world class presence on the web. Other strategies for using the internet are discussed in chapters 11-13.

Internet Marketing Overview

The internet offers small business two opportunities: first, to significantly increase sales through an online channel of distribution, and second, to increase the efficiency of business operations. Both opportunities should help to drive higher profits and customer service.

Almost all national retail organizations today have an internet site where anyone can place an order. Most are even able to accept credit card payment for instant processing of an order. In fact, there are some companies that accept orders solely from the internet. Following are case histories how a few companies have used the internet to increase their sales.

Office Depot

In addition to e-commerce sales (selling direct from their web site, Office Depot has gone a step further than their competition. The company has included perks for their contract customers. Specifically, they have linked the website to their ES9000 mainframe, enabling customers to get their own specific contract pricing. The closest any competitors have come is storing customer's shipping information. The result was $67 million in sales in a recent year. That doesn't come close to an internet-only retailer like Amazon.com, but it is a phenomenal success for Depot's first year in the internet market.

Increased sales revenue is not the only benefit that that Office Depot's marketing plan has reaped. A new level of efficiency has also been reached. The leading benefit that has created such efficiency is the number of online customer orders that Depot does not have to:

1. Take up more of a salesperson's time on the phone.
1. Take up an order-entry clerk.
2. Waste time trying to understand precisely what the customer needs. (The customer can browse though the company's entire catalog of merchandise.)

Instead, the company's time can be spent on more important customer service issues. A salesperson can get out in the field to meet one-on-one with their customers. Order-entry clerks can spend more time making sure they key exactly what the customer wants. That covers the benefits to the company, but how about the customer? Are they benefiting as well? Customer feedback has been overwhelmingly positive. This is mainly true because internet ordering is an additional service, not a replacement of service. Some customers in the past would complain that they couldn't speak to a Real Person when they needed to most. Now when they need to place an order, there is no need to speak to someone unless more clarification is required, and when it is, there are usually Real People available to speak with.

Cannondale Bicycles

In early 2005, Cannondale Bicycle Corp, a manufacturer of high-end bicycles, was looking for new ways to engage more directly and interactively with its customers to strengthen its brand and help drive sales. Cannondale saw an opportunity to take advantage of the through the internet.

"In taking advantage of this new social media and facilitating community, we are able to build on our brand's cult following, producing new products based upon consumer input, and, perhaps more importantly, promote cycling as a lifestyle."

To get started, Cannondale created a company blog operated by "Brad," a pseudo-employee and longtime Cannondale Headshok icon, who would comment about company developments and respond to customer questions. The company saw this as a more personal and interactive way to interface with its "hard-core" customers and provide an alternative to its current customer service department.

"One of the key benefits that we've seen through the Brad blog is the ability to acknowledge and respond to technical, product-related questions directly and less formally, and post the answers in an open forum for others to see and comment on. The biking community immediately latched onto the information and shared the link around the Web, driving traffic to Cannondale's site.

Cannondale is also using blogging technology to connect externally with its retail partners. The company has an e-commerce site where its retailers go online to order products and facilitate communications and discussion between the retailers and Cannondale's dealer service group.

Cannondale's foray into blogging has been more successful than the company first imagined, and has gone beyond the tangible benefits of improving relationships with its customers and retailers, increasing sales and improving the corporate brand.

Laser Eye Surgery Clinic

A laser eye surgery clinic offered the latest technology in LASIK and PRK, two of the most popular procedures for the correction of near-sightedness, far-sightedness and astigmatism.

However, it was believed that the web site needed a new look in order improve conversion (percentage of visitors who actually inquire or buy). In addition, the web site was not well placed on search engines. Over one year consultants worked closely with the eye laser firm to provide search engine optimization, advice on web content and design and to streamline the sales processes. As a result, Unique Visitors increased over 500% over a one year period as first page listings on Google and Yahoo soared.

Advantages of E-Commerce

E-Commerce is conducting business with customers online. E-Commerce provides many benefits to small businesses, as well as larger firms and organizations. Following are some of he advantages:

1. Increased Customer Base and Sales - Increased business can be achieved by expanding marketing over the internet. Online sales transactions are increasing almost exponentially as more and more consumers are making purchases on line. Your physical location becomes irrelevant and your marketing area can extend globally if you desire. In addition, the internet is used as a research tool to collect information about products and services and retailers prior to visiting a brick and mortar establishment.

2. Strengthen Customer Relationships - A company's achievement is built around its dealings with its customers. The stronger the relationships, the higher the success. E-commerce improves the boosting of these relationships. It mechanizes the sales process so that customers can simply answer the questions they have in a simple and one-to-one way.

3. Lower Costs - E-Commerce can drive order costs do*wn*. Research indicates that the average cost of electronic orders range from $10 to $75 per order. By mechanizing the order procedure online, a company can lessen these costs from $2 to $5 per order, which is a noteworthy profit for the company (Parker, 2004).

4. Increased Marketing Power - E-Commerce helps companies promote their products quicker and boost the products demand, by offering the entire essential information about them, including product as well as design details, metaphors, pricing and delivery information, category and accessibility of products. The customers can access this information on a 24x7x365 basis. This verity saves *the company's precious time and increases customer satisfaction. Some say that this is the main value of e-Commerce.*

Customers are in a situation to manage the way they shop by allowing themselves to balance products on an on-demand base, checking the given product information as well as saving precious time.

5. More Flexible Pricing Models - Through e-Commerce, a company can generate diverse price models based on the wants of each one of its customers. For instance, a customer is in a place to visit the web store, find his/her way through its departments, place an order and pay in a manner based on condensed prices specially defined for him/her only.

It is really not too difficult to build a world class presence on the World Wide Web at a fairly small investment. You can spend as much or as little as you want. Following is an overview of the steps involved in creating or increasing your e-commerce capabilities.

How to Easily Build a Competitive Presence on the Web

This discussion will provide the basic steps toward developing a presence on the web that will allow you to compete more effectively with larger businesses. While you need to do additional reading and possibly employ the services of a creative and competent professional, following are the basic steps and best practices to follow.

1. Benchmark the Competition – First of all, make a <u>quality commitment</u> that your web presence convey to consumers that you are a reputable, important and viable alternative to larger companies.

To do that, begin by making a list of your competitors, large and small. Include companies that you may not directly compete with in your market area but who are the most successful and "best in class." Then study their websites, print copies of the best, make notes on content as well as look and feel. For each one, surmise the:

- Purpose of each competitive web site
- Business objectives, direct sales (e-commerce)
- Target audiences
- Primary selling message
- Support for their sales propositions—price, service, incentive, etc.
- Structure of site
- Content & visuals
- Personality & brand character
- Key words used to generate traffic
- Strengths & weaknesses of site
- What opportunities do competitive sites present to you?

2. Determine the Purpose of <u>Your</u> Website – Given that you want a website that is very competitive with those of larger companies, and considering what you have learned from researching the best competitive sites, what is the <u>purpose</u> of your site? Informational? E-commerce? What is your <u>main selling idea</u> on the site? What products and services should you offer? What competitive advantages can you present? Why should consumers looking for what you sell buy from you rather than Goliath? What should your site "be like?" What content can you offer?

3. Initial Organization & Copywriting – After you have determined the structure and basic content of your site and the specific pages that will be included, write a rough draft of the copy for each page. At minimum, you will have pages for:

- Home page
- Products & services
- About us
- Site map
- Privacy page
- Ordering/shopping cart/payment

Your home page, in a sense, will be the most important page on your site because it will be the "landing page" for your visitors who will only spend a few seconds there before deciding whether to look further on the site. The home page needs a strong headline, supporting copy, and illustration.

4. Design – Now that you have a rough draft describing what exactly your web site will say, it is time to actually design the look and feel of the site, including graphics and illustration, layout, typography, links.

You can do the design work yourself with existing, low-cost software, which includes templates where you "fill in the blanks" and provide illustrations. Most major web hosts also offer free software permitting you to do web design.

The alternative is to hire a web designer to design the site for you based on your direction (recommended unless you are proficient in web design). Hiring a highly qualified firm or individual need not be very expensive, and they have technical, programming, and creative expertise that most of us don't possess. (Note: many web designers are registered on freelance sites such as guru.com and elance.com, and they will bid on your projects.) You would provide the designer with the URLs of the websites you have benchmarked and your copy. The designer will submit their creative work to you in stages for your approval and changes.

5.   Reserve Several Domain Names – Your website will have a special address on the internet called a URL ((Universal Resource Locator), e.g., www.AdMediaStore.com. It is recommended that you reserve several or many domain names. Any web host will do this for you for free or for a nominal cost (or search "domain names"). Your domain name should ideally:

- Define your product/service using words consumers would use to search for what you offer (and that the search engines will index and fine)
- Be easy for surfers to remember
- Be no more than 63 characters!It is likely that many of the names you would like have been reserved by someone else, so you need a good list of alternatives. (Note: if a domain name with ".com" at the end is taken, it may be available as an .org, .biz, etc.)

6.   Select a Hosting Service – A web hosting service will provide your gateway to the internet, and it will provide the necessary storage for your website.

There are dozens of good, inexpensive hosting services (e.g., 1&1.com or StartLogic.com) at a cost of less than $10.00 per month (normally paid one year in advance). If you have an e-commerce site, there are specialized hosts from which you may choose, e.g., EZMerchant (www.bizwiz.com/merchant/application.htm) for under $100 per month. As you compare alternative hosting services in terms of what they provide and cost, you should expect them to include:

- Disc storage – 800-1000MB
- Transfer bandwidth – 40GB
- Domain registration – Free or nearly free
- Allowed sub domains – 10+
- Email accounts – Unlimited
- Control panel – Included
- Web content generator – Included
- Customer support – Phone & email
- Set up fee – Free
- Monthly fee (12 months in advance) $7.50 – 10.00+

7. Optimize Web Site for Search Engines – Ideally, you would like to be in the top 10 results of a Google/Yahoo! search, which is extremely difficult to accomplish, but being in the first several pages may be achievable.

In part, the key search engines—Google, Yahoo!, MSN, Ask.com—will find your website based on the key words with which the pages in your website are associated. If you have the technical expertise you can do this yourself, your web designer can do it for you (assuming they have the expertise), or you can hire an outside Search Engine Optimization (SEO) firm to help you. At minimum, best practices include:

- Choose key words that describe your website offerings—and which people would most likely search—offerings and make sure that these words and phrases are amply represented on your pages.
- Create HTML meta tags for each web page that the search engines will also consider in their searches.
- Without ruining your copy, up to 5-10% of the words on each page should be key words which will help improve your search engine ranking.
- Also use keywords in the links on your pages, e.g., rather than saying, "home page," use a key word phrase instead.
- Get other websites to link to your website as search engine returns are influenced by these links.

8. Go Live! – Your website is written and designed. You have a domain name, the site is optimized for search engines to find it, and now it is time to upload the site to your host server. Again, you can do this yourself or your website designer or webmaster can do it for you.

If your website was created with a web-authoring tool, the HTML version must be uploaded into the host account using the File Transfer Protocol (FTP) function.

9. Submit Your Site to the Search Engines – After your website is live, it must be registered with the search engines so that they know it exists. This is basically submitting your URL to the engines, especially, Google, Yahoo, MSN, AOL, Ask.com.

Since over 80% of website traffic comes from search engines, it is vital that the engines are able to find your site when someone types in one of your key words.

You can manually submit your site to search engines or hire a firm to do it for you; there are many paid submission services like Addpro.com, which includes manual submission to the most important engines and online submission to 1,500 others.

In addition, you should submit your website to online directories, like "The Open Directory," www.dmoz.com .

10. Promote Your Website – Finally, it is time to generate target audience visitors to your site. There are many tools you may use. The following some highlights:

- *Links.* As mentioned previously, developing links from other websites to yours will raise your rankings with the search engines, especially Google.

- *Press Releases.* You can send out press releases announcing news about your business and referring people to your web site. You can send releases to media yourself, especially in your market area (e.g., local newspapers, even TV and radio stations. In addition, for a nominal fee, you can utilize a press release distribution service like prweb.com (there are many such firms) that will distribute your release to traditional media as well as search engines, e.g., Yahoo! News, and will email it to their members who are interested in your category of news. In addition, it provides additional links with your key words that can show up on search results. I highly recommend this tactic.

- *Submit Articles.* You can also provide articles (embedded with your URL) to webmasters who have specialized editorial related to your business area. They are hungry for content, and their readers may click on your embedded link, which will take them to your website.

- *Email Newsletters.* You can publish a useful newsletter that you can email to your customer list and your website visitors who have opted in to receive your newsletter. Electronic newsletters are much cheaper than printed newsletters and can be extremely effective in driving traffic back to your website. Do not spam people with your newsletter. It could get you blacklisted and kicked off your host service. A newsletter is a project you could do yourself, or you could hire a specialist to write it and handle the distribution for you.

- *Advertising.* You can advertise on line or off line to generate website visitors.

Offline, use media targeted to your market area or trade publication with your web address. Be sure to include your web address in all of your advertising, direct mail, stationary, business cards, etc.

Online, you can place ads in e-zines, or buy ads, banners, or links on websites or networks of websites that reach the same type of people you do.

◆ *Pay-per-Click Advertising(PPC).* One of the most important and cost efficient ways to generate website traffic is to "advertise" on pay-per-click (also known as cost-per-click search engines. Google is by far the largest PPC engine, followed by Yahoo!, MSN, and dozens of others.

The signup process is very simple. For example, to sign up for Google's AdWords program, simply go to adwords.google.com, provide the typical registration information, and select the language and geographic area you want to target (world, countries, U.S., or your specific local market). You will be prompted to write one or more brief ads that people would see when doing a Google search for one of your key words. You will be asked to provide a list of as many key words as you want along with your bid for each. Generally, the higher your bid vs. competitive bidders, the more clicks you will get. You will also be asked to specify your monthly budget.

For example, let us assume that one your key words is "Edsel." A surfer does a search on Google for the key word, "Edsel." When the search results come up, at the top or bottom of the page is your ad: **Edsel Owners – parts and service at discount prices.** The surfer clicks on your ad and is redirected to your website. You pay Google the amount of your bid for the clicks that Google delivers.

Google offers several targeting options and is always coming up with new ideas for this type of pay-for-performance advertising. Currently, Google is testing pay-per-sale— where the advertiser would pay Google a fixed amount for conversion that is shown on your AdWords pages.

Like everything else, nothing is ever as simple as it seems, and so it is in trying to maximize ROI from PPC advertising. You can either study up and do it yourself, or you can hire a professional or agency to help you. (Note: Google offers online training, as do other PPC search engines.)

Promotions. Special promotional offers communicated in your ads and on your website can often increase your click rate.

11. Analyze Results & Continuously Improve – One of the great things about marketing on the internet is that most everything is quantified for analysis. In your CPC programs you will be able to easily tell which key words are generating visitors/clicks to your site and which aren't. You can tell which of your ads is pulling best. You can also determine your conversion rates by ad and key word so that you know which key words and ads are most profitable. In addition, the audience data available on your control panel provides an enormous amount of results and diagnostic information to help you improve your performance—either your website structure/content or the marketing and promotion of the site.

12. Improve Conversion Rates - Conversion is the percentage of web site visitors who take some desired action, such as buying a product. It is important to get consumer feedback on your web site covering: content, ease of navigation and usability, image projected and so on. Based on consumer feedback you can continuously improve your site's effectiveness in providing leads and sales-- and at a relatively low cost to you.

***

For a small business, the internet can be a great equalizer vs. large businesses. Consumers across the country and around the world don't know that you are a small business because your website should make you look just as important, successful, and credible as those Goliaths.

Effective use of the internet is vital to competing in a global marketplace. Your web presence can be very professional and competitive, yet low in cost. And it can produce incremental sales and profit results for you.

Chapter 10
Review

1. Think of some new ways you could potentially increase your business, revenues and profits through the internet.

2. Look at your internet presence through the eyes of a larger competitor. How would that competitor describe and evaluate your internet presence?

3. Look at your web site through the eyes of a target consumer. How would the consumer describe and evaluate your site?

4. Has your site been optimized for search engines? Do you use the right key words? Are there more key words which you could test?

5. What is your marketing plan for generating targeted traffic to your web site? For closing the sale among those who landed on your site?

6. Are visitors coming to your web site from your trading area or where?

"The future of advertising is digital."

--Bill Gates

Chapter 11

Free Marketing in Social Media

Initially used as a way for family and friends to stay in touch and share, social media are now fast becoming an important marketing tool as well. A vast majority of Advertising Age or AdWeek issues devote significant space to various aspects of social media and marketing. Social Media Ad Agencies are popping up, and Advertising agencies-- like Campbell Ewald-- are adding senior social media marketing specialists to their staffs.

Social media also help organizations manage their public relations challenges. People in public relations constantly monitor the social media to identify any impending crises or trends in public opinion. Even small businesses are jumping aboard.

Introduction to Social Media

Definition of Social Media

There are many different definitions of social media. Some are technology oriented and some are rather confusing. Instead of referring back to the popular definition found on the Wikipedia, a better definition, in my opinion, is one by Joseph Thornley, CEO of the PR firm Thornley Fallis. (Joseph Thornley, "What is Social Media?" 2008.)

Therefore, social media are those in which the users create the content and are interactive, regardless of the communication platform.

"Social media are online communications in which individuals shift fluidly and flexibly between the role of audience and author. To do this, they use social software that enables anyone without knowledge of coding, to post, comment on, share or mash up content and to form communities around shared interests."

Examples of Social Media

Some of the more popular social media applications are listed shown below.

+ ***Blogs.*** Blogger, LiveJournal, Open Diary, TypePad, WordPress, Vox, ExpressionEngine, Xandi

+ ***Micro-blogging / Presence applications.*** Twitter, Plurk, Tumblr, Jaiku, fmylife

+ ***Social networking.*** Bebo, Facebook, LinkedIn, MySpace, Orkut, Skyrock, Hi5, Ning, Elgg

+ ***Social network aggregation.*** NutshellMail, FriendFeed

+ ***Events.*** Upcoming, Eventful, Meetup.com

+ ***Wikis.*** Wikipedia, PBwiki, Wetpaint

+ ***Social bookmarking (or social tagging).*** Delicious, StumbleUpon, Google Reader, CiteULike

+ ***Social news.*** Digg, Mixx, Reddit, NowPublic

+ ***Opinion sites.*** epinions, Yelp

+ ***Photo sharing.*** Flickr, Zooomr, Photobucket, SmugMug, Picasa

+ ***Video sharing.*** YouTube, Vimeo, sevenload

- *Livecasting.* Ustream.tv, Justin.tv, Stickam
- *Audio and Music Sharing.* imeem, The Hype Machine, Last.fm, ccMixter
- *Media & Entertainment Platforms.* Cisco Eos
- *Virtual worlds.* Second Life, The Sims Online, Forterra
- *Game sharing.* Miniclip, Kongregate

This chapter focuses on examples from different categories: Micro-blogging (Twitter), Social Networking (Facebook, MySpace), Social Bookmarking, and Video Sharing (YouTube), and others.

Social Media in Marketing

As stated earlier, Social Media were initially by used by individuals for personal purposes. Social media were and are a great way to stay in touch with family and friends, networking, sharing information and opinions on blogs, posting photos, and more. **But** now, social media are rapidly developing into an important marketing tool.

However, *Social media marketing* is the process of promoting your products, site or business through social media channels. Social media are developing into a powerful marketing tool that will get you links, gain more exposure, draw attention, generate more traffic, and close more sales.   There is no other low-cost promotional method out there that is as effective in generating a large number of visitors, some of whom may become repeat visitors to your web site.

Whether you are selling products/services or just publishing content for ad revenue, social media marketing is a potent method that will make your site profitable over time.

Role of Social Media in Marketing

While social media are obviously not the single panacea for marketing ailments social media can play an important role in the marketing communications mix for many companies, both in terms of branding and web site traffic.

1. Branding - The focus of advertising and marketing communications planning is currently shifting from passively "reaching" a target audience with a mass message (e.g., via a commercial within a television program or on a radio station) to *engaging* the consumer on a deeper level. The key to engagement is *relevance* of message and media to the audience.

2. Web Site Traffic - While web site traffic objectives aareintertwined with branding objectives, social media can also help drive a large volume of targeted traffic to the advertiser's website. For example, as will be discussed later, to generate traffic to your website, you can join relevant groups, post relevant messages about your products or articles, aggressively develop your network, and more.

Furthermore and maybe best of all, the cost of this traffic is minimal because the initial out of pocket cost of social media is so low (primarily overhead, cost of computers, and time). Of course, if advertising is used, there is cost. Following is a brief discussion of several leading social media sites:

Twitter, Home of Tweets

What is Twitter? Twitter (www.Twitter.com), one of the top 50 sites in terms of worldwide Alexa traffic, was founded by Jack Dorsey, Biz Stone, and Evan Williams in March 2006 (launched publicly in July 2006). Twitter is a social networking and micro-blogging service that allows users to post their latest updates-- which are limited to 140 characters. The updates are called "tweets" and can be posted in three ways: web form, text message, or instant message. The company has been busy adding features to the product like G-Mail import and search. Twitter also recently launched a new section on its site called "Explore" for external and third party tools to interact with Twitter and a new visualization tool called Twitter Blocks.

Twitter as a Marketing Tool - For businesses/marketers, Twitter is another channel which connects and engages current and potential customers with your product or brand. It allows deeper infiltration into the values and lifestyles of interested participants, which should help build marketers build customer satisfaction and brand loyalty.

Kate Kay of ClickZ wrote about Twitter as a marketing tool in December 2008. "It's been called a tech-geek fad, a business flop-to-be, and waste of time for most marketers, she said, "but the fact is big name brands are on Twitter. While detractors argue brands don't even belong on the quick messaging platform, they are there -- from Ford to Dunkin' Donuts to Whole Foods. They're engaging in experiments with customer service, branding, and corporate culture-building in the decidedly public forum."

"Some see Twitter as an extension of the marketing department, she continues, "others view it as a customer service tool, and some say it's best for corporate communications."

Before joining Ford Motor Company in July as its global digital and multimedia communications manager, Scott Monty reportedly had a good following on his personal Tweeter account. "I wanted to get down and personal with people," said Monty, who believes Twitter enables that more so than Facebook, MySpace, or blogs. Getting personal made sense for Ford, which, according to Monty, hopes to "humanize the brand." (ClickZ)

Beyond branding, Twitter is also a **traffic generation tool**. The placement of links within profiles and conversations can direct visitors to specific website(s), and is "especially powerful if you are targeting early adopters and influencers."

As a **lead acquisition tool**, Twitter doesn't always reach the audience you want. Most Twitter users are somewhat web savvy, and it is sometimes difficult to target a specific subset of the general demographic and determine their level of potential interest

Twitter's Audience - What is Twitter's audience? Is it really a major factor in the media marketplace? As mentioned earlier, Twitter, according to a Wikipedia posting, is the 50th largest web sitge in the world as measured by Alexa.

Twitter's recent user growth has been nothing short of phenomenal. The rise of Twitter has been the talk of the tech and media worlds. In 2008, Twitter's users grew 422% and another 1,382% by early 2009.

By June 2009, according to internet audience research firm, *com.Score,* Twitter reached 44.5 million users worldwide, 20 million of whom are in the USA. So, Twitter's audience is larger than the audience for a decent prime time network TV program delivers.

According to Hitwise data, Twitter's demographic profile is quite different than that of Facebook or MySpace.

Demographic Profile of Twitter Users

- 63% are males
- 26% are 35-44 years old
- 15% of Twitter visitors are "Stable Career" types, comprised of a "collection of young and ethnically diverse singles living in big-city metros like Los Angeles, Philadelphia and Miami." The Stable Career group tends to work in the arts and entertainment industry, drive small cars and espouse very liberal political views.
- 12% of Twitter's visitors are "Young Cosmopolitans," 40-somethings who are more likely to drive a Prius, earn

household incomes over $250,000 per year and identify with very liberal politics.

Also, according to Hitwise, Twitter is no longer dominated by the 18-24 age group - middle aged men are now the key drivers! This may be in line with Twitter moving from being a *'my cat's been sick' status reporter*, to being used more widely as a distribution network and feed reader.

How to Start Using Twitter to Market - Learning how to use Twitter is simple. So, let's start at the beginning, then move to some smart tactics and best practices. Here is what you have to do first to start Tweeting and growing your business.

1. ***Sign up for Twitter.*** As The first thing you have to do is sign upfor free (at www.twitter.com). Twitter is a social networking site that is referred to as 'micro-blogging'. It involves the use of up-to-the-minute updates to share with others doing what you are doing. Since Twitter is free, all you need to do is create an account to get started. Create a profile that outlines what you do. Include information relevant to your products that readers will find useful and interesting.

2. ***Follow Prospective Customers.*** A large Twitter following is a powerful way to increase website traffic with relatively little effort. Find like-minded people who may have an interest in your product or those that may have a problem your product can solve and start following them. People have the tendency to follow someone that follows them, so you the potential to quickly build a large following.

3. ***Update 'Tweets' Regularly.*** Update your micro-blog posts or 'tweets' on a regular basis to keep the content fresh. Tweets are limited to 140 characters, so keep it concise and to the point. Your tweets can include a link to your website along with a

comment that may stir the interest of your potential customers. Use tweets to advertise specials and offer helpful tips relating to your products.

4. ***Post an Eye-Catching Picture.*** The image that you post on Twitter will be seen next to your tweets and will serve as an icon for your profile. It doesn't have to be a picture of you; it can be of your company logo, a product, or of any image to your liking.

5. ***Put Twitter on Your Website.*** Twitter offers badges that you can insert on your website so that your site visitors can see what you are doing and follow you on Twitter if they are not already doing so.

6. ***Keep Growing Your Following.*** Once you begin to create a following on Twitter, you will watch it grow each day. The more people read your tweets, the more people will see your website link, and in turn you will start seeing an increase in website traffic at an unbelievable rate.

Follow the above Twitter strategies to build a targeted audience following, keeping with the adage, "quality not quantity." You will be able to tell who the best tweeters are, the ones that get mentioned a lot, the ones that have spent some effort setting up their backgrounds, and add a lot of value. Next, we will get more specific with suggested tactics and best practices.

Facebook

Facebook is a *global social networking website* that is operated and privately owned by Facebook, Inc. Users can add friends and send them messages, and update their personal profiles to communicate with friends and colleagues. Plus, users can join Facebook networks organized by city, workplace, school, and region.

While a student at Harvard, Mark Zuckerberg founded Facebook with his college computer science buddies, Eduardo Saverin,Dustin Moskovitz and Chris Hughes. Initially, The Facebook's membership included only Harvard students, but was eventually expanded to other Ivy League, schools and Stanford University. Later Facebook was opened up to any university student, then high school students, and, finally, to anyone aged 13 and over

Facebook has met with some controversy. It was blocked intermittently in several countries-- including Syria, China, and Iran, although Iran later unblocked Facebook in 2009. Facebook has also been banned at many places of work to discourage employees from wasting time communicating back and forth with friends. Privacy has also been an issue, and it has been compromised several times. Facebook is also facing several lawsuits from a number of Zuckerberg's former classmates, who claim that Facebook had stolen their source code and other intellectual property.

Facebook as a Marketing Tool - From a marketing standpoint, Facebook represents a potentially powerful viral marketing opportunity for marketers aiming at either younger or older groups.

Facebook Users - A January 2009 *Compete.com* study ranked Facebook as the most used social network defined by worldwide monthly active users, thus overtaking MySpace. Facebook reportedly hit *300 million users worldwide* (reported September 2009), half of whom use every day.

- Potential Global Audience – 300 million users and growing
- Potential U.S. Audience – 150+ million
- Increasingly balanced demographics for a broad range of
- products and services
- Maximizing marketing impact with Facebook requires doing a lot of things right (see Tactics & Best Practices).

Facebook User Demographics - From a media standpoint, Facebook obviously represents a huge potential audience. The difference between the <u>how</u> audience is generated by a television program vs. Facebook is important to understanding the nature of social media. For example, the audience generated by a television program is accomplished from the top down-- by the corporation in its selection of program content, talent, time period, and so on. Facebook's audience, on the other hand, is generated by the users creating and sharing content.

The *demographics* of Facebook users still skew toward women (56%), 18-24 year olds of college age, but *most of the growth is among 35+ year old users*. For example, while 41% of users are 18-24, the growth rate among the 35-54 year old demo is growing fastest (September 2009. vs. six months prior) with a+276% user growth and 194% growth among the 55+ age group.

Power of Viral Marketing - Facebook has a huge user audience with enormous viral marketing potential-- some users have generated millions of web site visits! Viral marketing is basically "spreading the word" through others. For example, if you begin with 10 "friends" who each get an additional 10 friends to your web site, each of whom gets another 10 friends to your web site, it is possible to generate millions of visitors or customers.

Facebook Costs - In terms of costs, Facebook, by most any measure, would be extremely cheap. Primary costs involve computers, staff time, and any optional advertising or promotion done on Facebook or on other sites. This is not to say, however, that there isn't a lot of "sweat equity" involved in the "free" claim. Managing a significant social media program can be quite labor intensive.

Putting Facebook to Work - Facebook can be used to find new customers, stay in touch with existing customers, promote new products or services or to serve as a near perfect customer service medium. Facebook provides users access to many functions and applications.

Today thousands of business owners and professionals thrive online because they know the secrets of using Facebook, which offers unprecedented opportunities for the large corporations and the individual professional alike.

MySpace

What is MySpace? Like Facebook, MySpace is a social networking website. Its headquarters is in Beverly Hills, California, where it shares an office building with its current owner, Fox Interactive Media (owned by News Corporation). MySpace became the most popular social networking site in the United States by June 2006, but by April 2009, according to *com.score*, MySpace was overtaken internationally by its main competitor, Facebook, in terms of monthly website visitors.

MySpace vs. Facebook - There seems to be some confusion about whether MySpace is basically just another Facebook. Although there are some similarities, in actuality, these sites look and function quite differently. It is important that anyone looking to utilize these tools is aware of the differentiating aspects of the sites. So what are the differences?

1. *Profile Presentations* - First, MySpace profiles are all unique; users can incorporate a variety of colors, photos and flash applications to their pages. On the other hand, Facebook's profiles are clean and uniform because Facebook uses a template design that cannot be modified (as it can be in MySpace).

2. *Audience Differences* – MySpace is popular with both the high school and young adult age groups as well as with the over 40

group-- with an average user age of 35. *Quantcast* reports (10/09) that 57% of MySpace users (in the U.S.) are female, 26% are teens, 46% are 18-34, and 26% are over 35. MySpace users tend to be below average in income and college education.

3. ***Site Etiquette is Different*** - On MySpace it is more socially acceptable to "friend request" or message random people. On Facebook that almost never happens, and it is considered border-line offensive. Facebook friends are generally people you actually know.

4. ***Functionality*** - Once you have figured out all of the basics, you can begin to familiarizing yourself with the really important differences — in functionality. Both sites have different applications and capabilities that make them unique and the more you know about them, the better you can think creatively about how to apply them to your particular client or business. MySpace's three unique functions are the bulletin   board, blog posts, and music applications.

5.***Profile Presentations*** - First, MySpace profiles are all unique users can incorporate a variety of colors, photos and flash applications to their pages. On the other hand, Facebook's profiles are clean and uniform because Facebook uses a template design that cannot be modified (as it can be in MySpace).

6.***Audience Differences*** – MySpace is popular with both the high school and young adult age groups as well as with the over 40 group-- with an average user age of 35. *Quantcast* reports (10/09) that 57% of MySpace users (in the U.S.) are female, 26% are teens, 46% are 18-34, and 26% are over 35. MySpace users tend to be below average in income and college education.

7.***Bulletin Board*** - The first, the ***bulletin board***, allows users to post messages which all of their "friends" will see upon login. Because of its visibility on the homepage, it is a quick and easy way to send messages to all of your friends at the same time.

8.Blog Area - The second, the Blog Area, appears on each profile and allows users to make blog posts without actually posting a blog.

9.Music -- And, finally, My Space's most effective function is the ability to add music to your profile-- great for musicians

On the other hand, Facebook's applications are a phenomenon that have taken on a life of their own ever since its introduction. *Facebook now has many more applications than MySpace.* But the key is to be aware of the tools you have and to recognize that these sites are more than just a profile with your picture and some basic info. In the end, the more you know about the apps from both MySpace and Facebook, the smarter you can use them.

MySpace as a Marketing Tool - While declining, MySpace remains a very important marketing tool for certain marketers, especially if used in combination with Facebook.

Audience - MySpace has about 100-125 million total users world wide and 75 million in the U.S. The number of MySpace users has declined somewhat with the growing popularity of Facebook. Monthly users are estimated to have declined from about 65-66 million U.S. users in April 2009 to approximately million monthly users in September 2009.

Demographics - Demographically, MySpace users are more likely to be female, and are still quite young (26% 13-17 and 46% 18-34). Users are also more likely to belong to an ethnic group, especially Hispanic. Because of their ages, no doubt, they are below average in income and college education. (Source: Quantcast)

Potential Marketing Applications - MySpace can create an additional presence on the web especially for marketers who cater to MySpace's largely younger audience. Since MySpace is affiliated with MSN, anyone who uses Windows Live is more likely to find your "space."

Increase website traffic with MySpace by networking with people who have similar interests (i.e. have a problem that your product can solve) and provide a link to your website on your space. Also, reflecting back on the demographics of MySpace users, the network might be most relevant for products and services consumed by young consumers, particularly teens and the 18-34 group. On the other hand, some bloggers voice the more enthusiastic view of MySpace as represented below:

> *"MySpace is not only for teenagers and musicians. MySpace is also making a buzz among Internet marketers. At the invitation of Internet marketing guru Marlon Sanders, I set up a profile to see what the buzz is all about. Marlon calls it "...a 'secret' networking method the people on the inside are using." Being the active experimenter that I am, once I got started, I couldn't stay away from MySpace, setting up my profile, posting on my blog, adding events to public calendar. As I poked around, I thought about how this networking space could work for professionals as a business tool. It's pretty easy to set up a profile and it's free. If you're using it as a business tool, be professional about the information you reveal. Remember MySpace is ultimately a SOCIAL tool and many people use it to hook up for dates and relationships. If that's not your intent, keep your content business-oriented.*

> *What I noticed in looking at random profiles is that most are sloppy and incomplete. A lot have no information about the person and no photo. What's the point? My sense is that a lot of profiles get set up and then abandoned, much like blogs.*

YouTube

What is YouTube? - YouTube is a video sharing web site on which users can view, upload and share videos. Three former Paypal employees created YouTube in February 2005. YouTube began as a venture-funded technology startup, primarily from a $11.5 million investment by Sequoia Capital between November 2005 and April 2006. In November 2006, YouTube, LLC was bought by Google Inc. for $1.65 billion, and is now operated as a subsidiary of Google. The company uses Adobe Flash Video technology to display a wide variety of user-generated video content, including movie clips, TV clips, and music videos, as well as amateur content such as video blogging and short original videos. Most of the content on YouTube has been uploaded by individuals, although media corporations, including CBS the BBC and other organizations, offer some of their material via the site, as part of the YouTube partnership program.

Unregistered users can watch the videos, while registered users are permitted to upload an unlimited number of videos. Videos that are considered to contain potentially offensive content are available only to registered users over the age of 18. The uploading of videos containing, pornography, and material encouraging criminal conduct is prohibited by YouTube's defamation rule. Accounts of registered users are called *"channels* .

You Tube as a Marketing Tool - YouTube has become an extremely important marketing tool for individuals, companies, organizations, and even politicians. Certain videos go viral and catch the attention of the national press which exponentially increases exposure of the video. YouTube has developed a huge audience and offers an effective communications tool which anybody can use (no doubt to the displeasure of the broadcast television networks).

Audience - According to data published by internet researcher, *com.score*, Google received about 6.4 billion video views in January 2009-- about 43% of all videos viewed on the internet. YouTube accounts for 99% of

Google's video views Also, according to You Tube, people are watching hundreds of millions of videos every day on YouTube-- and uploading hundreds of thousands of videos daily. In fact, every minute, ten hours of video are uploaded to YouTube.

Demographics - YouTube's user base is "broad in age range, 18-55, evenly divided between males and females, and spanning all geographic areas. Fifty-one percent of users go to YouTube weekly or more often, and 52 percent of 18-34 year-olds share videos often with friends and colleagues. Commercial Message. "With such a large and diverse user base, YouTube offers something for everyone." (Source. YouTube)

YouTube as an Ad Medium - The Association of National Advertisers (ANA) is extremely concerned about the declining effectiveness of broadcast television, or at least their perceptions of the decline. What is disturbing to broadcasters is the significant decline in expenditures in broadcast television even before the 2009-2010 recession.

***

Advertisers are actively looking for more cost effective alternatives which still provide the communications benefits of video-- sight, sound, and motion-- but in a much more targeted manner.

Consequently, more and more companies are using You Tube as a marketing tool where video clips can be hosted for free and people can view the clips for free. The service is so popular that Google recently purchased it for $1.65 billion. In fact some diehard users have stopped watching TV altogether and they prefer spending time watching videos on YouTube. So given its massive popularity, innovative marketers look at it as a perfect opportunity — a free opportunity — to showcase their offerings over there.Just to give you an idea of the potential media value offered for free on YouTube, some videos have generated over 50 million views.

If you bought 50 million impressions on one of the commercial broadcast networks it could cost up to $1,000,000 or more!

Another example, the Obama Girl's video (03:18) generated an estimated 3.4 million views, worth around $68,000, plus a huge volume of free publicity in all of the mass media. It's not very difficult to increase the popularity of your videos over YouTube. The more people who view your video, the higher your popularity grows, and nearer your video goes to the top page, the home page. Once you have uploaded the clip you are given some code that you can use to embed the video into your own blog or website. Even if just 300 people visit your blog everyday there is a probability that 200 will watch the video. You can also increase the views by putting the video link in your email signatures and on all the websites you have.

Then there is a cascading effect. The more people watch it, the higher the video moves, the higher the video moves, more are the views it gets…and so on.

In order to get decent views make sure your video is interesting and worth watching. If you produce a lousy video it could adversely affect your marketing efforts and people may start relating you with the bad video they watch. And also be careful about the copyright violations you may inadvertently commit. Produce your own videos, don't record them from.

Making Videos - Just by using a garden variety video camera you can create small clips and then upload them to YouTube. If you can edit your video, you can also embed your URL somewhere unobtrusively in the video. Of course, higher end video cameras, lighting, sound, and editing equipment would be worthwhile for serious film makers. Just remember that, regardless of equipment, ***content is king.***

It is interesting that the National Association of Broadcasters (NAB) in 2009 talked about TV Production in the Age of YouTube. "Lo-Fi, Hi-Style is about making beautiful content with low-cost gear. In the end it's not the equipment ..." In other words, the idea is far more important than how elaborate the production is.

YouTube.com is not too complicated to use. In fact, the opposite is true. YouTube.com is easy to master. The website allows just about anyone to sign up for an account, upload, share video clips, and view other people's video clips.

YouTubers and potential YouTubers would be advised to steal some of the production planning disciplines from large advertisers who have video production down to a science. For example:

- Determine the length you want the video to be.

- Develop an integrated video and audio script (write it down!)

- Plan out a second by second "storyboard" for the video, showing what the audio and video is supposed to be by second.

- Use the "storyboard" as a template to produce the video. On the cautionary front, there are some no-nos:

   * Do not upload any TV shows, music videos, music concerts or commercials without permission unless they consist entirely of content you created yourself. The Copyright Tips page and the Community Guidelines can

help you determine whether your video infringes someone else's copyright.

* Despite this advice, there are still many unauthorized clips from television shows, films and music videos on YouTube. YouTube does not view videos before they are posted online, and it is left to copyright holders to issue a takedown notice under the terms of the Digital Millennium Copyright Act.

No Videos Required Option - Don't have a video? Don't want to make one? No problem. If the thought of producing and airing a good video on YouTube is scary or intimidating, there is good news-- you don't have to produce your own videos to get started on YouTube and have an active social experience. You should will likely overcome your apprehension and publish videos that can connect you with your market, but you don't have to start there. A few things that you can do without producing video content of your own include the following:

* Comment (on others videos, or channels)

* Share (more on that later)

* Create play lists of your favorite YouTube videos

* Rate videos (1-5 stars)

* Favorite videos (another playlist)

Toward More Effective Videos - Try the following:

1. *Sharing valuable content.* For those who are familiar with the various sharing options found on many blogs and social

networking sites, you'll be glad to know that YouTube has this function as well. YouTube users can now share a video using one of the popular social networking sites (including Twitter); it also can be sent to one of your YouTube friends, or emailed. YouTube also allows you to embed video content for a single video, a playlist, or a channel.

2. ***Social activities update feeds.*** While not comprehensive as Facebook or other feed activity updates, with the release of *realtime updates*, YouTube seems to be trending in that direction. The fact that this feature has been introduced along with other recent enhancements, there may be other activities will be streamed out as well.

3. ***Understand your video's effectiveness.*** One of the challenges with social media sites is the difficulty in measuring the effectiveness of social media activity. Understanding how the market responds to your content can help video publishers provide relevant content to grow their business and increase sales. Besides getting feedback from video ratings and user comments, there's Insight Statistics and Data.

4. ***Gain Insights.*** YouTube's reporting function helps you understand views, viewer demographics, popularity, and community.

5. ***Community.*** The community tab of Insight reports on how other YouTube users are interacting with your video contents in the form of rating, comments, and favoriting. Used properly, this information can drive future content you publish, making it more relevant and targeted.

6. ***Hot Spots.*** The Hot Spots feature is available on a per video basis, and helps you understand the attention your video has at any point, compared to videos of similar length. Learn where

you are loosing interest, and make appropriate adjustments in future videos.

No other social networking site provides this kind of data for free. Let's hope they continue to build on these useful reporting features!

Website Traffic & Conversion - Active YouTube users generate interest in their profile (Channel) page, and this generates traffic to their website (assuming you are naturally peppering links in your channel and video descriptions).

While According to one YouTube user, while "Google remains the number one traffic generator for my site, traffic coming from YouTube users are joining my site for access a special report at 357% the rate of those coming straight from Google search, as the second highest conversion source (Twitter is #1)."

"What this tells me, is that having YouTube as a part of a social marketing strategy is not only valuable, but serves as a very important source of website traffic that converts (opts-in)," he continues.

Blogs

Nobody seems to know how many blogs and bloggers there are. Millions blogs and millions of bloggers on every subject imaginable— from politics to business and advertising to cooking and, interior design and furniture, foods and health, space and science, lawn care, cars and trucks and auto racing, sports, and about anything else you can think of.

Why Blog? -A "blog", abbreviated word for weblog, is a web-based journal in which people can publish their thoughts and opinions on the Internet. It is everyone's home on the world wide web and probably their number one venting venues.

Blogging is the easiest and quickest avenue for non–coders to get their message online. Most blog services are even free for casual or non–

demanding professional uses. Individuals and companies publish blogs for a variety of reasons; some blogs are launched for marketing purposes, others are posted just for fun. Here are a few things you can do with a professional blog:

1. *Product Promotion* – Many individuals and companies use blogs for free marketing. Posts can be created as product reviews, articles, news or whatever. You can also link your blog to your corporate or sales sites.

2. *Customer Education* – Blogs can be used to inform customers. corporate blog can contain product news, tips, company news, articles and more to educate customers or shareholders about products, services or corporate happenings.

3. *News and Information* - Numerous blogs are used to relate current events. Some bloggers publish national news and commentary; others use blogs to cover local events.

Blog Services - Blogging can be a highly personal endeavor, so you will want to look for a blog site that suites your needs. Some blog tools are tied into personal pages whereas others are integrated with social networking. On the other hand, other blog services are intended for professional use and include the ability to customize templates, monitor visitors and track referrers.

So when looking for a blog service, pick one that offers you the kind of exposure you want and complements your level of expertise. Below are some criteria that can be used to evaluate Blog Services:

1. Blog Design Tools - The top blog sites offer an assortment of templates and tools to customize blog entries, including the capability to add photos and sidebar links. Services ought to offer tools for experienced coders as well as non–coders, such as the ability to compose posts in code or through a text editor.

2. Promotion/ Tracking Tool -A number of sites host their own blog site with a directory, other blogging services facilitate blog design and submit your blog to several directories. A few also offer tools to help you track visitors, referrers and comments.

3. Ease of Use - Frequently blogs are composed and posted by those that do not code, so it is necessary that the service be simple enough for all levels of expertise.

4. Technical Help/Support - Since many blogging sites are free, technical support is principally limited to online documentation like FAQs and a searchable knowledge-base. However, the best sites also post tutorials and a weblog that covers help topics For the easiest to use, free blog service we could find, see WordPress.com. Or if you are interested in working with code, see Blogger.com (owned by Google).

Marketing Role of Blogs - The growth of online research before purchasing travel services is certainly not a new trend. For years we have seen significant growth in online shopping, but the most notable trend is the emphasis on consumer generated content and how it influences purchasing decisions.

With Universal Search and the emergence of blended search results, blogs have become even more common and their role has become twofold; marketing and technical. Primarily, blogs provide a forum for communicating local information to your customers and allowing them to interact. This opens up communication and provides many consumers with the candid information they are seeking when researching travel. This is one of the main marketing benefits.

Secondly, blogs provide a Search Engine Optimization benefit. By housing fresh content (much of which is consumer generated), you may also benefit from improved visibility in the search engines. Consumer generated content is advantageous technically, as comments provided by your guests provide the fresh content that the search engines view (and rank) favorably

Are Blogs an Important Marketing Tool? - "How have you used blogs in your business? How significant a role has blogging played in your marketing efforts?" Here are the comments of one business-owner-blogger:

"Is blogging significant? Blogs have changed my business completely. When I realized what a powerful tool blogs could be for businesses, I dove in head-first. Patsi and I studied TypePad in depth and taught a teleclass for coaches about how to set up a blog. That turned into a blog about blogging (this blog), then it evolved into an ebook, Build a Better Blog, then it became a TeleSeries called Conversations with Experts (Paul Chaney was our very first guest and since then we've done 62 Conversations!). Next came consulting and training and setting up blogs for clients. A whole new business was born and Patsi and I officially became The Blog Squad and business partners, merging our two businesses into one in July 2006, nearly 2 years after we started blogging.

"Blogs are not my only marketing tool, but a primary one. We have 10+ blogs. Each has a different purpose, whether as a private training system, a private membership blog for clients only, for the public to learn more about blogs, Internet marketing and ezines, or as a way to focus and feature a specific project. Blogs have extended the reach of my business in ways I could never imagine.

"I've met more amazing peoplethrough blogging in the past 2 years, than in the prior 8 years of working online. More joint ventures have happened, speaking gigs have materialized, publication opportunities... I could go on and on. Suffice to say, blogs have changed my business AND my life, for the best."

How to Start a Blog - Anyone can start a blog. It's straight-forward and, in a lot of cases, free. Here are the steps:

1. ***Select a Blogging Provider*** - The first step is to find a good blogging provider that appeals to you. The most popular providers include WordPress.com, Blogger, TypePad, and Xanga as well as others These sites offer pre-made templates and push-button publishing that don't require a lot of technical know-how. Following are examples of three leading providers

- **Wordpress (****)**

   Promote, inform, amuse or even rant to the far reaches of your brilliance, with WordPress.com. This blog service is fitting for amateur and prolific bloggers alike and is uncomplicated to use. WordPress.com is a free blogging service inspired by the users of WordPress.org, who requested an easy to use, hosted blog service. WordPress responded by launching WordPress.com. This service is simple, hosts your blog, submits your blog to the Goggle blog directory and monitors your stats; in essence, this is an all–inclusive free blog package.

Unlike many free blog services, the Wordpress service does not load your blog with ads and WordPress is all about blogging, they are not trying to double as a social networking site. This service gives you every tool you need to build and promote your blog; additionally, WordPress.com is the only free service we found that gives you referrer stats without having to add a third–party application

- **TypePad (***1/2)**

Watch your stats, promote your blog and make money with TypePad at less than $5 per month for the basic membership. TypePad offers advanced tools like statistics, word banning, text file uploads and you can publish an About page.

Typepad is a good tool for bloggers that are looking for exposure; this service can submit your blog to Google, Technorati, FeedBurner and more. If you want to keep your blog private they also support private and password protected blogs. Unlike many free blogs, TypePad does not put ads on your site unless you request them

This service is comparable to WordPress, but doesn't obtain the number one spot, because it is not free and they offer few customization features without upgrading to their Pro package.

- **Blogger (***)**

Get the word out, with Blogger! Share your life, your product or your ideas *for free* with this blog service. Blogger has given the world a voice and offers endless template configurations.

Blogger launched in 1999, was bought by Google in 2002 and is one of the most popular free blog services. Since they are owned by Google, they make it easy to sign up for adsense and they automatically submit your blog to the Google blog directory so your blog is available to millions.

We liked Blogger because it is easy to use, yet is flexible enough for advanced users who want to build their own templates. The only drawback to Blogger is that you have to add your own traffic tracking devices if your want to monitor your visitors.

2.*Choose a Design Template* - Once you sign up, you'll have a gallery of ready-made templates to choose from. With these, you can pick a color scheme and layoutforyour blog. Most sites come with a set of predefined layouts and schemes that you can choose from. Select one and personalize it. Then add your name, interests, images, etc. If you want to, get a more unique template, there are some sites up that have many of these that might make it look better. For example, PimpMyProfile.com or Pyzam.com.

3.*Customize* - Add blogging freebies like buttons, images, blog chalks, imoods, tagboards (for example, myshoutbox.com), guest maps, guestbooks, comment boxes for readers' input, etc.

4. *Private of Public?* Decide whether you want your blog to be private or public: do you want any Internet visitor to be able to read your blog, or do you just want your friends and family to be able to read it? Most blog sites offer the ability to password-protect your published posts so only those who you approve of can view what you've written

5. *Test & Improve* - After you've set up your blog, write a few posts to test it out, and make any adjustments to the layout or style that you see fit. Like if you just got a new template, you'd check your blog to see if you like it, right? At first, it will seem tough to figure out what to write, but once you get into a routine of daily blogging, you will find it addictive. Write about your day, your thoughts, events, ideas, fears, pleasures, the news, current affairs, art, or anything you are interested in!

6. *Build a Blogging Circle* - Visit other blogs to build a blogging circle. When you leave comments, add your blogging address so they can visit you too. (Note: This will not work if your blog is private)

7. *Build an Audience* - Publish your blog by sending the URL to your friends or publish the URL on your website. Add the URL to posts you make on other blogs. Register URL with search engines.

***

Social media can be a free or low cost marketing strategy for small business. This chapter has reviewed some of the more popular social media sites, but there are many others you may wish to also consider, such as Yahoo: Answers, Digg, LinkedIn, StumbleUpon, and many others.

A disadvantage of social media is that properly attending to the execution can be very time consuming. An alternative for some might be to assign individual employees to individual social media.

Chapter 11

Review

1. Why should a smallish business have an important presence on the world wide web?

2. What social networks make the most sense for your business? Why?

3. What are the important differences among Facebook and MySppace?

4. What are the advantages and of having a blob for your business? What could you do to make it interesting to others?

5. What is the marketing value of YouTube to your business? What could you do to generate a million views of your video?

On Guerrilla Tactics

"Low-cost, creative strategies

allow you to fight and win

in today's marketplace."

--Industry Week

Chapter 12

Creative Media Tactics

*"**Winning** requires thinking outside the box."*

Beyond the use of traditional media such as television, radio, and print, small businesses may also benefit greatly from non-traditional use of traditional media—or cost effective non-traditional media alternatives. Many creative uses of media can yield great increases in cost effectiveness and results.

Chapter 12 provides a sampling of 91 "thought starter" ideas that small business advertisers may consider and adapt to their particular needs.

Broadcast Media

1. Use the Most Cost Efficient Day parts – Use only the *most cost-efficient TV day parts* (e.g., day parts with lowest target audience CPMs/CPPs). (Note that the CPM averages by day part vary by up to 300%.)

Which day parts make the most sense for you, of course, will depend on who your target is. However, as an example, if your primary target is female homemakers, daytime television is three times more cost efficient than prime time in reaching women. And daytime radio is more efficient than drive times.

2. Use Only the Most Cost Efficient Programs – Within your selected day parts, select only the most cost efficient individual programs. (The efficiency of programs within a day part varies by 100% or more). For example, in a recent primetime upfront, "Idol" sold at a CPP of $35,000, and "Shark" sold for under $20,000. If you are trying to get more bang for the buck, why would you spend 170% more to have spots in Idol.

If you have selected the most efficient television or radio day part for your buy, the next step is to rank order the available shows by CPM based on your target audience. Negotiate the best prices and commercial positioning and buy only the most efficient programs. Remember, higher-rated programs are not more effective (recall) than lower rated ones, so the tendency to pay more a premium for them is emotional, not rational.

3. Try Shorter Commercial Lengths - Try reducing the length of your radio or TV spots. A 60-second spot costs twice as much as :30, but won't get twice as many viewers or recallers. If your message can be communicated in :30 or less, going with shorter spots will allow you to run more ads which normally pulls more customers. It's better to be there every day with small ads than every month with one big one.

4. Piggyback Two :15s - Buy :30 positions and piggyback two :15s in the time slot. Normally, if purchased independently, "15s would cost 60-70 percent of the :30 rate. But if you buy :30 positions and piggyback two :15s through scheduling, you will only pay 50 percent of the :30 rate. If you piggyback :15s, the commercials need to be distinctly different commercials. A :15 will normally get 70-80% of the recall of a :30 at 60-70% of the cost, but this one tactic could provide 140% of the recall at the :30 price.

5. Buy Opportunistically! - Let the stations know that you will buy their unsold time at the last minute. Give the stations your buy specs and ask them to call you when there is a last-minute opportunity. (You may even wish to hold a percentage of your budget back for opportunistic buying). However, if you don't follow through and buy on occasion, stations will stop coming to you with offers.

6. First Five Seconds is Crucial – If you use broadcast media, the first five seconds of your commercial are the most crucial to its success. The commercial must immediately get the consumer's attention, but do it in a way which is *relevant to the product.*

7. Negotiate "Value Added" With Stations -- When you are ready to place orders with television or radio stations, make your offer contingent upon their providing you with the requested FREE merchandising assistance. Radio stations, particularly, are good at helping you with promotional ideas-- which could include on air promotions, remotes from your place of business, golf outings for clients, tickets for sporting events or just additional spot announcements and billboards, and much more.

Co-Op

8. Fully Capitalize on Manufacturer & Supplier Co-Op Programs - Make sure you use all of the co-op advertising dollars your manufacturers and/or suppliers make available—at least for the programs which support your marketing strategy. Co-op programs usually split the cost between manufacturer and retailers in most media—as long as certain guidelines are met and proof of performance is provided for reimbursement.

9. Get Vendors to Share Ad Costs - Split advertising costs with the vendors who sell to you and who would also benefit from a shared program with you. At the very least, ask vendors to pick up part of the ad cost in exchange for displaying their logo or product information in your ads.

10. Co-Op Mailers & Statement Stuffers - Find other companies that have a similar target audience that mail out a lot of invoices and packages. Place your ad in their mailings, and in return, they place their advertising in your mailings.

11.   In-Store Cross Promotions - If you are a retailer, find other retailers with which there would be mutual benefit from in-store cross promotions, e.g., a pizza restaurant and a movie theatre offer. Each business would display point-of-sale material, offers, etc. from the other.

12.   Share Ad Space – Complementary products or services could share space and cost of advertising for cross promotions. For example, if you sell milk, you could partner with a cookie or cereal company. The partners would share ad space and cost. In broadcast, partners could share :30 commercials (e.g., :15 and :15). Also check to see if one of your manufacturer co-op programs would pick up even more of the cost.

13. Horizontal Co-op – If you share space with other retailers—such as in a shopping center, consider forming a co-op committee or a merchant's association. (You have to set up a legal entity to do this.) Each store would contribute an agreed upon percentage of sales to the merchant association budget to use for traffic building promotions which would benefit all members. A larger budget would permit the association to do major promotions and media programs not affordable to most individual businesses.

Direct Marketing

14. Solo Direct Mail - A letter and brochure before customer contact can increase business. An IBM study concluded that selling time can be reduced from 9.3 to 1.3 total hours with direct mail advertising. A sales and marketing executives international study showed salespeople went from eight orders per 100 cold calls to 38 orders per 100 when direct mail was used.

Direct mail results depend largely upon the quality of the list and the effectiveness of the mailing package. The CPM for mail is much higher than you'll pay for print ads, but if you create a finely tuned list of recipients, you can reach more highly qualified prospects.

Few small firms are qualified to do their own direct mailings, so find a reliable specialist to do the work for you. Interview at least three or four mailing list vendors before you commit your money to a direct mail campaign.

15.   Outbound Telemarketing – This can be a relatively low cost way to generate sales leads, set sales appointments, or help close a sale. Also, research has found that when direct mail is followed up with a phone call, the results increase dramatically. Telemarketers charge in a variety of performance models or as low as $30 per hour.

Flyers & Brochures

16.   Flyers are the Thrifty Entrepreneur's Dream - You can create them very inexpensively on your computer, or your local print shop can print them for you. You can use as much color as you like, with either a color printer or old-fashioned colored paper stock. Pack them full of information and post them on every bulletin board you can find that will allow you space.

17. Stuff Flyers in Bills or Other Planned Mailings --Easy to distribute in bulk, these handy attention-getters can also be used as bag stuffers or inserts to put in with billings or to include when mailing payments to your suppliers. In fact, don't mail anything out of your business without including some little sales piece. Take advantage of piggybacking on that postage stamp. Placing stacks of flyers in building lobbies and tucking them under windshield wipers are done frequently, but you must be willing to alienate some people if you use these methods of distribution.

18.   Get a Quality Four-Color Brochure A brochure will allow you to provide a lot of detail about your product or service. Simple three-fold brochure stock may be purchased from mail order suppliers such as Paper Direct in small quantities. This type of stock comes in attractive cuts and colors. Template software can be obtained that permits you to use your computer to generate classy looking brochures at minimal cost. Make your headline stand out. Use clip art or graphics. Give your customer as much quality information as you can pack into this identity piece. Keep it up to date and personalize it when possible (by writing in the margins or underlining specifics that might interest a particular prospective customer). If you have a slightly bigger budget, go for a slick four-color piece. You'll need a printer who can do four-color separations, so if you're in a small town market with few hi-tech services, you may want to call a national firm that specializes in doing short runs. Firms such as Kinko's and AlphaGraphics do high quality, low-cost work for small businesses. They also have a wealth of samples to get your creative ideas flowing.

19.   Endorsements & Accolades - If someone says or writes something good about your product or service, put out reprints and let the world know how good you really are. Have them available and visible inside the business or frame it if it is a big deal! Get endorsements from friends, neighbors, and customers!

20.   Door Hangers – These can be very effective and are widely used by fast food and home delivery and service businesses. If you choose this medium, don't scrimp on the stock. Make it heavy so it won't blow off doorknobs and litter the neighborhood. Add a coupon or some other incentive to your copy. Door hangers are a good way to focus in on a specific target buyer.

21. Print First Class Business Cards - Print attractive and informative business cards that include your logo and hand them out everywhere, consistently! If appropriate for your business, you can use your card as a discount certificate or other incentive. Or, you can have it placed on a magnetic backing so that it (hopefully) winds up on a refrigerator. If you use letterhead stationery in your business, have it match your business card. Keep your identity as consistent as possible.

22. Get a Toll-Free Phone Number - It makes you look more professional and encourages business—and the fees aren't as high as you might think.

Online

23. Make Sure Your Web Site is as Effective as it Can Be! - As discussed previously, it is imperative that your web site represents your business in a clear, professional, and compelling manner. It is always a good idea to test web sites with consumers to uncover any problems that would reduce its ability to project the proper image or convert your visitors to prospects or purchasers.

The internet provides you with an opportunity to look important, successful, and credible! On the internet you can look and act like Lexus... at very low cost. Develop an e-commerce capability in order to sell world wide, capture leads, and provide customer service. Do business online. *See Chapter 10.*

24. Add Audio or Video to your Web Site -- When a visitor has the ability to listen to an audio message or watch a video, perhaps from you, research suggests that your conversion rate should improve (all else equal).

25. Submit Your URL to the Search Engines Monthly - Submit your web site's URL to major search engines like Google, Yahoo, Bing, and others. In some cases you will also be able to submit key words and a description of your site. If the search engines are not indexing your site, you will not get visitors.

26. SEO Optimization - Being ranked high on search engines is perhaps the most important part of having a successful business. The best way to raise your rank on search engines is through SEO optimization. It is important to optimize your web site by putting keywords on your web site that are specific to your niche. Maximizing your search engine ranking is the most important part of running a successful and profitable web site. , if you lack the expertise or are not able to work on your web site yourself, hire an **expert.** Remember, the web site traffic you generate from these organic searches is FREE.

27. Use Pay per Click Search Engines - One of the easiest ways to generate web site traffic is through PPC programs available on Google, Yahoo, Bing, and most other search engines. The process involves writing an ad which appears on search results pages based on key word searches. You bid on key words which you feel your target will be searching; when someone searches one of your key words, your ad may be revealed at the top, at the side, or at the bottom of the page. If the surfer clicks on your ad, he/she will be taken to your web site. Each search engine will provide you with reports of which key words are clicked and how many conversions resulted with cost per click/conversion.

28. Local and Regional Targeting - In your pay per click program, target and pay only for clicks in your primary market area. Google, Yahoo can schedule your ad listings to appear only to people searching in a particular state, city, or region. Now it's easy to target online customers within, say, 25 miles of your front door.

29. Local Business Ads - Get noticed on Google Maps. People searching for information related to your business will see your location, contact information, and an image of your choosing highlighted on a map of your area.

30. Local Yellow Pages - Customers use internet Yellow Pages services everyday to search for local products and services. Getting your business information in their database means that more customers can find you. Many basic listings are FREE. (Local.com, Google.com, Yahoo.com, Switchboard.com, Superpages.com)

31. Email – Email can be a great customer relationship management tool (CRM) by allowing you to stay in contact with your customers at almost no cost! First, make sure you collect customer email addresses. Email your customers special offers at least on a monthly basis. Also, on your website, you can collect addresses of people who would like to be kept informed of your products and offers or would like to receive your newsletter. Use a do it yourself email company to build and send professional looking emails at a very low cost.

32. Podcasts – Podcasts can expose your company or product to new audiences. They can also create traffic for your website and establish valuable back-links. Podcasts can be used as on online advertisements for your business-- busy showing-off your business and products while you are hard at work. By submitting podcasts to specialist directories and even the *iTunes Music Store* **Podcast Digital** can provide valuable links back to your website and business. Companies like *Podcastyourbusiness.com* and *talkshoe.com (business podcasting)* can provide you with assistance in planning and scripting your broadcasts, production, hosting, and audience generation.

33. Generate Ad Revenues from Your Web Sites – If you choose to do so, you can generate some ad revenues from your site by allowing Google and/or Yahoo put ads on your website and even your blogs. *Google Adsense* will pay you a share of the CPC revenue they receive from visitors who click on their ads located on your site.

34. Expand to Global Markets – On the one hand, you can target local visitors, but you your internet presence can also open up global markets for your products and services. You can let your ads run world wide or you can specify which countries you want your ads to appear in.

35. Mobile Phones – You will soon be able to buy video ads on mobile phone networks. Also, like Yahoo's sponsored search results on the Web, advertisers will bid in an auction on keywords that will display their ads on the search results page. The service will work on most mobile phones and handhelds that have Web browsing capabilities. Clicking on the link will take a user to the advertiser's mobile Web site or a landing page that offers more information, including the ability to call the advertiser, according to Yahoo. (In test).

36. Launch a Blog on Your Site and Update it *Daily*. - Nothing reads "I don't care" like a blog whose most recent entry is days old. Assign this task to employees who can write and spell—an illiterate blog is worse than no blog at all. Introduce people to your company and its staff. Highlight products. Run contests and give away company swag. Announce specials and upcoming product-line changes. Establish a "customer-of-the-month" tradition and do regular write-ups. Surely there's something you can say to your customers daily.

37. Start an Independent Blog – According to *Entrepreneur Magazine*, there are 100 times more blogs today than there were three years ago. Blogging is an opportunity to develop a relationship with your target market—on your blog and your postings on other related blogs. Best of all, blogs can be created and put online at absolutely no cost. Google offers this service free. Of course, you will have to spend time and probably some money to generate visitors to your blogs.

38. Post on Other Peoples' Relevant Blogs - Improve your credibility by posting comments on other relevant blogs-- like LinkedIn or Yahoo Answers.

39. Yes, use Social Networks! - Having a Facebook page may not earn you any new business, but *not* having one may cause customers to ask why you don't. Take some good pictures of your offices and your employees (unless you'd rather leave those details to your customers' imaginations), or, in some fashion, put a more human face on your company identity. Twitter is a young technology, and everyone's scrambling to figure out useful applications. In the meantime, let your customers at least follow you, have thought of on your own.

40. Online Listings - *B2B Magazine* found that 95% of purchasing agents surveyed said they use the web to research products and services. Local websites (local.com for example) offers vendors and businesses a free basic listing. Linking your website to complementary websites can generate potential leads. For example, if you own a print shop, submit your site to wedding-planning websites as a source for wedding invitations. Sign up at Yelp.com, which offers a free business page and allows you to interact with people looking for local businesses and services

41. Email - According to Forrester Research, 79 percent of consumers have signed up to receive e-mail at least from one company, and two out of three people surveyed said they read e-mail every day of the week. Use email to announce a sale, offer a discount, send a newsletter or invitation, direct customers to your website, and conduct a survey. Email generates immediate action: sales, downloads, inquiries, and registrations. Decision Direct Research found that the number of respondents who visited a Web site after receiving an e-mail promotion increased to 62 percent in 2007. The goal is to keep in touch with your customers, build relationships, loyalty and trust. **42. Saturate the World with Your Web Site Address** – Put your website everywhere—on notepads, pens, newsletters, bumper stickers, cups— anything you send or give away.

43. Article Marketing - If you write articles and then use a service to publish them, your articles can become viral. Your articles will spread like a virus and could have the potential to be viewed by hundreds of thousands of people.

44. Free Classifieds - Free Classified Adds are a great way to get free advertising without investing much of your time. Sites such as Kijii and Craig's List offer free classified ads in which you can promote your business nationally or locally. The only bad part about it is that your posts will disappear over time. This will require a little bit of extra time each week, but it is well worth it since it is a free method of advertising

45. Craig's List - From e-commerce websites to furniture wholesalers, small businesses both online and off are realizing the marketing power of Craigslist.org. Founded in 1996 by Craig Newmark, Craigslist.org gets an estimated 10 million unique visitors per day. With an online classified ads format organized by either region or city, Craigslist connects buyers and sellers in more than 300 communities; for the most part, posting on the site is free

 46. Targeted E-zine Advertising – E-zines are online magazines and newsletters and there are thousands of them. Ezines can be a cost effective ways to advertise your business.

Newsletters

47. Publish a Printed Newsletter - Publish a quality, useful printed newsletter for customers and prospects. The right newsletter can help establish credibility and professional image at a relatively low cost. Distribute your newsletter by mail and in your place of business. (You can do the newsletter yourself or you can hire someone to do it for you, but it must be an excellent ambassador for you.)

48. Publish an e-Newsletter - Publish an opt-in E-newsletter. People who subscribe to your newsletter have already consented to lending you their ear. Bend it. They are a targeted, ready-made audience waiting for you to solve all their problems. Help them do just that. You can use a third-party list manager such as Topica.com or Groups.Yahoo.com to manage your newsletter list, or you can self-publish.

Out of Home

49.   Digital Opportunities - Many digital innovations have come to the outdoor industry in the past several years, including brilliant, impactful boards where you can even digitally change messages on boards through out the country from one central location.

50. Zip Targeted Outdoor Posters – If you have certain zip codes or clusters that offer high potential, and you have a need for basic name awareness, consider buying 8-sheet or 30 sheet posters saturating your primary trading area with high visibility to local traffic.

51.   Mobile Billboards - MobileAds provides a fleet of billboard trucks to advertise your business and reach potential customers in territory that's uncharted by conventional billboards. MobileAds' Billboard Trucks are your answer to short-term advertising with messages delivered for any special event or service -- to just about anywhere you desire. Mobileads.tv

Public Relations & Publicity

52.   Send Out Press Releases – Frequent press releases are a must! They are free! Write and distribute press releases that are newsworthy, and send them to newspapers, magazines, and television and radio stations. If only one media outlet airs the story, you'll have free access to thousands of people. Design the headline to grab readers' attention in as few words as possible. Use active verbs. Get to the point quickly, with a lead sentence that will draw the reader into a convincing piece. Don't overlook sending your release to small local papers who are hungry for editorial material to use in their paper!

53.   Use Press Release Distribution Services - For free or for a small fee you can also submit your press release to a firm which will distribute your release to thousands traditional and web media and interested individuals. Your releases may also be indexed by Google and Yahoo! so that they may show up in searches of your key words. Examples of press release distribution firms include prweb.com, emediawire.com, and many others.

54.   Obtain Bookings on Interview Shows – Find something new or interesting about your business and expertise that you could talk about on TV or radio. For example, if you have a women's apparel shop, do a presentation on fashion trends for the fall.   If you sell toys, demonstrate the latest and greatest hot toys. Demonstrate how easy it is to put a business online.   Pitch the idea to stations.   Prepare thoroughly, don't ramble, stay on point, and rehearse. Make it fun and interesting for the audience.

Print Media

55.   Magazine Ad Remnants - Monthly magazines sometimes have unsold ad space at the end of the month they will sell at a discount (remnants). Let magazines of interest know of your interest!

56. Newspaper Ad Remnants - Newspapers frequently have last minute unsold space that you could potentially buy at up to 75-80% below their rate card price. You can contact the advertising sales manager yourself to let him/her know of your interest and that you would like to be notified when there is a remnant opportunity or you could place a standing order. Or, you can work with a middle man who specializes in newspaper remnants.

57. Incorporate a Direct Response Mechanism in Your Ads - For example, if you have an email address or an 800 number, put it in every ad for immediate response and feedback.

58. Test Classified Ads - Try advertising consistently in the classifieds or display classifieds. These ads may draw more customers per dollar than more expensive display ads.

59. Test Frequent Small Space Ads -Instead of a one-time big splash ad, be consistent with frequent small ads that work. Research has found that campaigns utilizing frequent small space ads can be more cost effective than few large ads.

60. National Magazine Editions in Local Market - If you want to use magazines but you are a single market advertiser, you can buy ads in local editions of most large national magazines, e.g., *Time, Sports Illustrated, Better Homes & Gardens*, etc.

61. Local Magazines Networks - Magazine Networks (MNI) is another alternative for advertisers who want the prestige of big national magazines in their local markets. MNI sells local market ads in networks of national magazines. For example, they offer business networks (*Business Week, Fortune*, etc.), entertainment, women/s, food, etc. (MNI.com)

62. Magazine Merchandising -- If your spending level in a magazine is sufficient, you may be able to negotiate some special FREE merchandising assistance from them. For example, they can mail copies of the magazine with a special cover and company information to a field organization, clients, etc. Magazines can also host golf outings or tickets and activities at sporting events, and a lot more.

Product Placement

63.   Movies, TV Shows, Print – Product placement is getting your product exposed in movies, TV shows, or other media. Product exposure growing by leaps and bounds. You might be able to expose your product or business in the media for low or no cost. You may not be the Cadillac CTS doing dare devil feats in the movie, *Matrix*, but you still may be able to get some product placement. Also, if you are in a local market, look at your locally produced programming on television, radio and print media. Talk to the media and take them an idea that would use your product on air. Or talk to a firm that specializes in helping companies get product placement, e.g., www.setresosurces.com.

64.   Game Shows – Ever wonder where the TV game shows get the products they give away as prizes? These prizes are a form of product placement incorporating a short "commercial." These sell for a small fraction of the normal rate, or perhaps up to $250 per exposure, not including product cost. This could be an interesting way to generate some national exposure at an extremely low cost. (As an example, see www.saveontv.com.)

Research & Assistance

65. Free Marketing/Media Assistance - Radio, newspapers and magazine specialists will frequently give free help in developing an advertising strategy. Just remember, they are trying to sell you something; do your own analysis & ask plenty of questions.

66.   Free Market & Media Research – Research, including market demographics, media information, money-saving ways to produce your ads etc., are available from most major local media, especially from your newspaper rep. Just ask!

Sales Promotion

67.   Use the Power of Free - Offer a valuable free product or service to people. Make sure your freebie is valuable as a stand-alone, but use it as a teaser that entices people to purchase something else. You should also require people to leave their email address before getting the freebie. This way you can follow up with them later.

68.   Print up Some Gift Certificates - These let your customers introduce you to new customers. Since you get paid up front for the product or service, these are cash-flow friendly.

69.   Send Greeting Cards - Birthday and holiday cards sent to clients could show your logo and remind them of your continued interest. Customer comment cards are also a great way to solicit feedback and involve your clients in your business.

70 Coupon Distribution – Distribute coupons in targeted zips and local neighborhoods. Examples of suppliers: Advo, Inc. – Super Coups (www.advo.com); Cox Target Media – ValPak coupons (www.coxtarget.com).

71.   Product Sampling – If you have a product that will sell itself it people just tried it, consider product sampling-- in-store or send samples direct to homes. Examples of suppliers: Sun Flower Group (www.sunflower.com) and Valassis (www.valassis.com). First Moments for expectant parents (www.parenting.com).

72.   Free Standing Inserts (FSI) – Target coupons or other offers to desired zip codes. Examples of good suppliers include: Valassis (www.valassis.com) and Goodway Marketing (www.goodway.com).

73.   Contests, Drawings & Sweepstakes - Periodic prize drawings can help create interest in a retail store or other business. Promotional materials like T-shirts, coffee mugs, or pens emblazoned with your logo also help spread the word.

74. **Low Cost/High Perceived Value Purchase Incentives** – Offer a high-perceived value purchase incentive to help close sales. Travel incentives—airfare, cruises, hotels for example—can be purchased for a few dollars. Make sure that your incentives are legitimate offers that will be an excellent experience for your customer. Another idea would be to cross promote with a nice **restaurant, e.g., offering free dinner for two or buy one, get one free. Be sure this offer is well promoted on site.**

75. **Continuity Promotions** – Not a novel idea, but onsite promotions aimed at getting customers to return to you with frequency are important. Many businesses give the customer a card which is punched with each visit or purchase—to get a free car wash, coffee, etc.

76. **Push Gift Certificates** – "Looking for that Special Gift for Someone? Choose one that is always right…in $XX denominations." Communicate via signage in store, at the cash register, and on windows. Offer shoppers an incentive to buy someone a gift certificate.

77. Leverage Media Merchandising - You can use media merchandising to implement a promotion. For example, if you are a car dealer, you could probably negotiate promotion support as a condition of sale. Negotiate this before you place your orders, not after, or you will not have any bargaining power.

Signage & Point of Sale

78. **Free and Low-Cost Point of Sale** - What will suppliers give you in the way of point-of-purchase materials, posters, stand ups, handouts, etc.? Some have excellent display racks you can use.

79. **Exterior signage** - National chains like Coke and Pepsi provide outdoor signs for businesses. There are also indoor lighted signs you write on with special markers to advertise your special off

Seminars

80. Could Seminars Help You Obtain Clients? If your business has know-how/knowledge that would be of interest to your target audience, consider conducting seminars in your selected market areas to help you prospect for new clients.

81. Sell Materials at Seminars – In addition to using seminars to build your awareness and reputation, they also provide an opportunity for on-site sales of books, tapes, and other materials.

Specialty Media

82. Increase Visibility With Specialty Media - Bumper stickers, balloons, buttons, decals, and even T-shirts are examples of ad specialty signage that work. Your local promotional supplier will have hundreds of examples of walking ads you can adapt to your needs. Paper or plastic bags and packaging make economical billboards too. Print your name, logo, and message on anything you can, on all sides. Don't miss an opportunity to get your word out. Mailing labels are a perfect medium. Everyone who handles your mail will see your ad at no cost to you.

83. Unique Corporate Gifts – Find something really special for select customers or prospects. For example, a TV station in Minnesota sends customers a package of Wild Rice every year (a Minnesota crop). A rep sent certain customers a high quality replica sword. Some send Trump steaks. Whatever it is, your gift must be very high quality, memorable, appreciated, and you must be remembered as the sponsor.

Trade Shows & Events

84 Trade Shows - Renting booth space at a trade show can be expensive, but the best shows are a great way to build your business. Have plenty of promotional materials ready to hand out to interested people. When the show's over, follow up. Call your leads in order of importance, but get in touch with all of them within seven days. Above all, keep every promise made at the booth.

85.   Community Events - Can you sponsor a community event? A fun-run, golf tournament, or other event that will be well publicized in the community? Your name may not be prominently displayed, but sometimes the positive exposure in the community will bring in new customers.

86.   Sponsor a Little League Team – Or volunteer at the Special Olympics or participate in the annual Rotary Club Christmas tree sale in your area.   Donate your product to local charities or speak to students at area schools about your business. All of these are terrific ways to position your company in a positive light in your community.

Other Ideas

87.   Get Your Product on QVC or HSN! The cable shopping networks have grown into multi billion dollar businesses selling everything from computers, inventions, jewelry, food, household items, apparel, and more. If your product survives their rigorous evaluation process, you could get airtime at no cost. You do have to provide inventory for them to warehouse and must generate hefty sales to be invited back.

88.   In-Store Advertising - If you sell impulse goods through supermarkets or mass merchandisers, consider in-store advertising or promotion such as in-store audio or video, shopping carts, cash register receipts, instant coupons, etc.

89. Shelf Talkers – These are small pieces of printed paper designed to be fastened to or hang from a retail shelf. They should be no more than 10 words with the product name and offer. The kind that bob, bounce or dangle seem to show the best results.

90.   Study Competitive Ads & Media – Study competitive ads and media. Especially watch what is repeated. Get on their mailing lists! Adapt and improve upon their good ideas!

91. Networking Opportunities - Attend meetings, events and tradeshows to meet potential customers. Every town has a chamber of commerce or business group. Even if you're not a member, you can still attend, network, hand out business cards, and build relationships.

***

You can generate a LOT of inexpensive media exposure and by using creative, low or no-cost media alternatives, targeted right into your Primary Market Area. The <u>quality</u> of the ideas you execute will be key.

__Think first class.__ For example, if you are going to have personalized T-shirts to sell or give away, make sure they are high-quality shirts!

Chapter 12 presented examples of 91 thought starters. Using this list as a starting point, it would be worth your time to brainstorm specific free or low cost ideas that could make a difference for your business.

Chapter 11
Review

Make a list of low-cost creative media ideas that could be applied to your business:

1. Broadcast:

2. Co-Op:

3. Flyers & Brochures:

4. Internet:

5. Newsletters:

6. Print:

7. Product Placement:

8. Promotion:

9. Publicity:

10. Seminars:

11. Specialty Media:

12. Sponsorships:

13. Trade Shows & Events:

14. Other:

On the Art of Negotiating...

**"In business,
you don't get what you deserve,
you get what you negotiate."**

--Charles Karrass

Chapter 13
Guerilla Media Buying

The Power of the dollar! Want to increase the purchasing power of your ad dollar? You have two opportunities to leverage your media investment.

As discussed, the first opportunity occurs when you are planning, strategizing, and deciding how, where, and when you are going to reach your target audience: which media, where, and when. Your plan may even include some of the low cost, creative media ideas from Chapter 11.

The second opportunity occurs when it's time to <u>execute</u> your plan. Then it is time to actually negotiate and buy the planned media in the quantities and quality needed in the right place and at the right time...and to do it all within budget.

Chapter 12 discusses some of the ways you can get more bang for your buck when you buy the media. We will discuss:

- *The art of negotiation*
- *Negotiating traditional media buys*
- *Guerilla media buying techniques*

The "Art" of Negotiation

SALESPERSON: This is a great TV program developed by the same people who did "Survivor." And the station is going to promote it as its #1 show. It is sure to do at least a 25 share and a 15 rating.

BUYER: You must be joking, Bill! Everybody and his brother are doing reality knockoffs. If the show is lucky, it will do a 20 share and a 10 rating. And I don't think it is worth more that $110 per point! What are willing to guarantee?

This is the type of dialogue you will have when buying media. Sellers and buyers are trying to convince each other of their points of view about the *value* of a media package.

It is important that you enter media negotiations with a good strategy firmly in mind. As the buyer, to a large degree you can control the negotiation process. If you have done your homework, know what you want, and understand the market conditions and media you will be dealing with, you are ready begin negotiating your buys.

Negotiating Strategy

To conduct a winning negotiation, you must have a winning strategy. If you conduct negotiations by the seat of your pants, you will likely be the loser in the negotiation. Following are the strategies we have found successful.

+ *Create a Win-Win* – *Everyone* who interacts with other people (buyers, sellers, spouses) should read Stephen Covey's book, *The Seven Habits of Highly Successful People*. In his book, Covey stresses the absolute necessity of creating a **win-win** scenario in negotiations.

    Negotiations can only occur when you have something the media want (your budget) and they have something you want (access to consumers). You need each other. Every successful negotiation that arrives at an agreement/deal has to be a win-win for both parties. If there is not a win-win, there will probably not be a deal.

Finally, don't be a naïve buyer. Understand that a seller isn't going to hand over $100,000 just because they like you.

- **Create a Strong Negotiation Incentive** – In order to get what you want in a negotiation: 1) you have to <u>know</u> what you want and why, 2) you have to have knowledge and information about the market and media, 3) you have to have some leverage—an incentive—for the other guy, and 4) you have to be willing to give up something that the other guy wants (compromise).

As stated above, you must create some incentive for the seller to agree to the deal you want (or close). If the seller already knows that they are going to get $XX of the budget, there is no incentive for the seller to make further concessions. But if the seller knows that you are only going to buy <u>one</u> station, and that he will get zero dollars if he doesn't do a certain deal, he will get motivated. The win-win would be that the seller gets ALL the MONEY and you get MORE AD EXPOSURE.

Important: You always need to have a Plan B (alternative) to pursue if a negotiation doesn't work out, whether you are buying television, radio, newspapers, or magazines or something else. Plan B provides you with leverage.

- **Don't Ask, Don't Get** – This sounds like a no-brainer, but buyers often don't ask...for something very specific. You might think that the newspaper won't give you two ads for the price of one, but unless you ask, with some rationale, you definitely won't get.

- **Conduct Yourself as a Professional** – Some media buyers scream and demean reps, throw tantrums and even physical objects. They are reinforced by a culture that thinks that media negotiators get what they want by beating up the reps with offensive behavior or not understanding that being a tough negotiator doesn't require being a jerk. Always conduct yourself

Negotiating Insights

We all negotiate in our personal and professional lives. We negotiate when we go to a garage sale, or when we want to do something different at work, or when we are dealing with members of the public. Sometimes it's easy to negotiate, but other times, when we have a great deal at stake or we are upset, the task can be intimidating or difficult.

1.   Overview of the Negotiation Process - Negotiating is the process by which two or more parties with different needs and goals work to find a mutually acceptable solution to an issue. Because negotiating is an inter-personal process, each negotiating situation is different and influenced by each party's skills, attitudes, and style. We often look at negotiating as unpleasant, because it implies conflict, but negotiating need not be characterized by bad feelings, or angry behavior. Understanding more about the negotiation process allows us to manage our negotiations with confidence, which increases the chance that the outcomes will be positive for both parties.

2.   Barriers to Successful Negotiation – Negotiation need not be confrontational. In fact, effective negotiation is characterized by the parties working together to find a solution, rather than each party trying to WIN the contest of wills. Keep in mind that the attitude that you take in negotiation (e.g., hostile, cooperative) will set the tone for the interaction. If you are confrontational, you will have a fight on your hands (James 2002).

3.   Trying To Win At All Costs – If you "win," there must be a loser, and that can create more difficulty down the road. The best perspective in negotiation is to try to find a solution where both parties "win." Try not to view negotiation as a contest that must be won (Benway, 1999).

4. ***Becoming Emotional*** – It's normal to become emotional during negotiation that is important. However, as we get more emotional, we are less able to channel our negotiating behavior in constructive ways. It is important to maintain control. (Belk 2005)

5. ***Not Trying to Understand the Other Person*** – We are trying to find a solution acceptable to both parties, we need to understand the other person's needs, and wants with respect to the issue. If we don't know what the person needs or wants, we will be unable to negotiate properly. Often, when we take the time to find out about the other person, we discover that there is no significant disagreement.

6. ***Focusing On Personalities, Not Issues*** – Particularly with people we don't like much, we have a tendency to get off track by focusing on how difficult or obnoxious the person seems. Once this happens, effective negotiation is impossible. It is important to stick to the issues, and put aside our degree of like or dislike for the individual.

7. ***Blaming the Other Person*** – In any conflict or negotiation, each party contributes, for better or worse. If you blame the other person for the difficulty, you will create an angry situation. If you take responsibility for the problem, you will create a spirit of cooperation (James 2002).

Guerilla Media Buying:
Traditional Media

The vast majority of media buys are negotiated for traditional media (television, radio, newspapers, and magazines). If you know what to negotiate for and you are good at win-win negotiation, and have a good incentive for the other guy, you can significantly increase the efficiency and cost effectiveness of your buy, i.e., more TRPS for the dollar.

Agency Commissions

The first opportunity, assuming that you handle your own advertising, is to recover agency commissions and cash discounts paid by the media—which you can then reinvest into media buys to increase your ESOV.

Commissions as Savings to You – Built into the rates of most media is a 15% commission for the ad agency. For example, if an agency places a $10,000 buy with a TV station, the agency pays the station $8,500, keeping $1,500 commission as its compensation. The media rate card will say: "15% commission paid to recognized agencies."

Since you are not technically a recognized agency, you may need to set up a separate corporation or LLC for the purpose of placing media buys as an agency.

Cash Discount – In addition to paying the agency commission, many media also offer a 2% cash discount for invoices paid within 10 days. This adds up to a total potential savings to you of **17%** on top of savings you incur when negotiating your buys.

Buying strategies vary by medium, so we will cover broadcast media (television and radio) and print media separately.

Broadcast Media

Broadcast media availabilities are perishable. Yesterday's unsold spot generated no revenue for the seller and no audience for any advertiser. (The time was probably used as a station promo or public service announcement).

Supply and Demand – As pointed out in Chapter 2, broadcast media prices are always a function of supply and demand. The seller (network or station) always wants to sell at the highest possible price, and the buyer always wants to buy at the lowest possible price.

When buying broadcast media, *timing can be everything*. Like commodities buyers, buyers and sellers of media are constantly trying to predict the market in order to determine whether to buy now or wait a little longer.

Here is an example of how quickly market conditions can change: We bought a primetime TV schedule in New York. After the orders were placed, the client decided that the media weight levels should be increased. One week later, prices for the exact same spots that we purchased increased by 75% - 110% because a lot of "new money" came into the market. The supply and demand dynamic drives pricing for networks/stations and dayparts as well as individual programs.

The Super Bowl is another example of supply and demand at work. The Super Bowl generated a 46 rating in 2010, which makes it the highest rated program in the U.S. But the network's price of $2.6 million per :30 commercial made the Super Bowl a very bad buy (in terms of cost efficiency). Nonetheless, the network was able to sell the Super Bowl out at $2.6 million because advertisers were willing pay the price to be in the Super Bowl, not because it was a good advertising value, but to satisfy management egos.

Another example is the difference in the CPPs paid by advertisers from program to program in the same daypart. For example, in the 2007 upfront, advertisers reportedly paid $12,000 CPP for a :30 spot in "NCIS" and $30,000 CPP for a :30 spot in "Survivor." This was purely supply and demand at work. But why would an advertiser in their right mind pay more than a 100% cost efficiency premium to be in "Survivor"? Don't make this mistake; be a value investor: buy into good shows with the highest discounts.

 Quantity vs. Quality – Network or station commercial inventory that is hard to sell or that is in high supply sells for less and vice versa. The following chart illustrates how one's media buying philosophy can result in paying low prices for "tonnage" or low demand inventory vs. paying a premium price for higher quality, high demand inventory:

Media Buying Philosophies

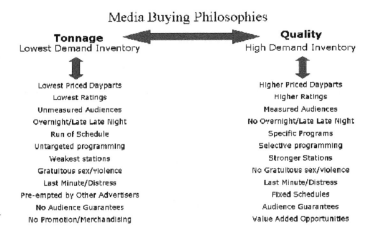

So, for example, as we noted above, the more popular primetime programs—with higher ratings—will typically sell at a significantly higher CPM or CPP because they are in higher demand among advertisers willing to pay the price.

The other side of the coin is that this creates a buying opportunity for advertisers who don't have an emotional need to be in the highest rated shows and who will take the risk of waiting until the last minute to buy unsold inventory at much lower prices. (Note: there is no relationship between rating size and commercial recall.)

Broadcast Negotiating Tips

Following are 10 tips for negotiating more value in your broadcast (television/radio) buys.

1. ***Bring Your Best Deals*** – Begin by calling ALL of the stations/reps that could make any sense. Give them your buy specs (outlines budget, daypart mix, programming guidelines, target audience, timing, etc.), and ask each rep for their best deals in terms of rates, quality, added value, and any other requirements. (Like car salesmen, however, media reps never give their best deal first.)

2. ***Have a High-Leverage Negotiating Plan*** – Develop a plan for negotiating your buy which will give you leverage over the sellers. Despite what the reps tell you, it is not necessary to buy many stations or even to be on the #1 station. For television, you need only to buy one good or two medium rated stations—as long as their target audience cumes are 70% or more for the day parts you are buying.

In radio, because the ratings are very small and most stations have cumes of less than 10%, you will need to buy enough stations to have a gross target demographic cume of 40-50% or more.

At this point, you should have called all relevant stations for their avails, and you have gone through several rounds of negotiation. Once you have reached the bottom line for all stations, tell them that you have decided to buy only "one" station. See if additional pricing or bonus spots are forthcoming.

If not, place the entire buy on the station with the best inventory, commercial positioning, and pricing. When you place the order, place it for 10-30% less or ask them to throw in some additional (specific) spots at no charge. More than likely, the station will accept your order as is, or perhaps they will suggest a compromise. Either way, you have gained ESOV!

This strategy is highly effective because it provides a win-win for both buyer and seller. The buyer obtains a higher quality, more cost efficient buy. The winning seller gets all the bucks, which is a big deal to station management.

   3.   Negotiate a Long Term Buy – Consider negotiating a 52-week buy, contingent on getting the programming/stations, commercial positioning, and lower pricing, which best reaches your target audience at below market prices. The broadcast and cable networks negotiate such buys with the large national advertisers in May/June. Your optimum timing would follow the upfront market if your "inside sources" think there are deals to be had, and you believe that advertiser demand will continue strong or increase as the year goes on.

Placing a long-term spot buy is a win-win with almost no downside for the advertiser. If the advertiser needs to cancel all or part of the buy later on, all that is required is two weeks' notice to the station. So the advertiser locks into a higher quality, lower-priced buy that he can cancel at any time—whether for financial reasons or to re-buy even better opportunities on this or other stations. And the station wins because it has future dollars on its books, which gives station management a sense of comfort.

4. ***Sweeten the Pot When You Place the Order*** – Let's assume that you have negotiated a buy with a number of stations in your market area. You feel that you can't get their pricing any lower, or their quality or value added any higher. You are ready to place your orders. When you do, call the rep and place the order at a lower price than what was last submitted. Chances are, the station will take the deal, and you just saved another 10% or more!

5. ***Get Audience Guarantees*** – The chances are, your sales rep will be trying to get you to up your audience estimates for their station/programs so they can charge you more. Always negotiate audience guarantees, so that if your buy doesn't generate as much audience as projected, you will get enough "bonus" spots to make up the difference and then some.

6. ***Improve Your Buy 100% with Every Make Good*** – When technical problems occur or the station pre-empts one of your spots for any reason, the station will likely offer you an equal value "make-good" spot. Tell the station that you will just take a credit, or you want make-goods which deliver *100%* more audience than the pre-empted spot. The rationale is that you scheduled the pre-empted spot as part of your marketing plan and were counting on the sales and profit that it would generate. The station left you high and dry, and you need to be compensated for the loss.

You will likely experience a lot of pre-emptions over the course of your schedule, so the added value from make-goods can add up.

7. ***Negotiate Added Value*** – You can negotiate added value with almost every broadcast buy. Added value can include bonus (free) spots, :05 billboards, ads on the station's website, remote

broadcasts from your place of business, traffic building promotions promoted on air by the station, tickets to sporting or entertainment events which you can use for customer drawings, etc. Many radio stations, in particular, employ promotion managers who can help you.

*8.   **Cultivate Information Sources (Reps)*** – Knowledge is power in this business, and the stations' reps know a great deal about supply and demand conditions, their inventory situation, market pricing, competitive moves and buys, etc. Take reps to lunch as often as possible. They will reciprocate with you. You will be able to use what you learn to improve your buys.

*9.   **Be   Ready   to   Make   Fast   Decisions   on   Buying Opportunities*** – If you have cultivated relationships with some key media sales reps and you have let them know that you are interested in "70% off card deals," be ready to approve a buy when they call. If you never buy anything, they will stop calling you.

*10.   **Commercial Positioning*** – Place your order contingent on guaranteed commercial positioning, e.g., first pod, first position in the pod, never within 15 minutes of a competitive spot. This alone could raise your ESOV by 20-30 percent!

Print Media

Buying print media is different than buying broadcast media. The nature of the medium is different, magazines and newspapers are used for different reasons, and the analysis/evaluation process is different.In addition, print media negotiations differ from broadcast media negotiations, as will be discussed below.

Print media have always published rate cards that show their rates in minute detail, e.g., by size of ad, coloration, discounts, etc., as shown on the following page.

Rate Card Example

Four Color

	Open	4 Insertions	8 Insertions	12 Insertions
1 Page	$100,960	$88,840	$85,830	$82,790
2/3 Page	75,380	66,350	64,090	61,800
1/2 Page	60,570	53,310	51,490	49,670
1/3 Page	39,030	34,350	33,200	32,010
2nd Cover Spread	226,140	199,000	192,210	185,420
3rd Cover	102,980	90,540	87,520	84,440
4th Cover	133,260	117,270	113,270	109,270

Two Color — Black and One Color

	Open	4 Insertions	8 Insertions	12 Insertions
1 Page	$85,830	$75,530	$72,940	$70,370
2/3 Page	64,090	56,410	54,480	52,540
1/2 Page	51,490	45,340	43,800	42,240
1/3 Page	33,200	29,230	28,220	27,230

Black and White

	Open	4 Insertions	8 Insertions	12 Insertions
1 Page	$68,640	$60,430	$58,360	$56,300
2/3 Page	51,270	45,130	43,600	42,040
1/2 Page	41,200	36,270	35,020	33,780
1/3 Page	26,540	23,370	22,580	21,790

Historically, most print media regarded their rate cards as Sacrosanct and would not "give deals" that would violate their rate card. However, in recent years business has been tough for print media—both newspapers and magazines—which have experienced declining circulation and share of market. Many believe that a lot of print media face extinction at the digital hands of the internet.

Large conglomerate advertisers with big print budgets changed print media rate cards forever when they consolidated their brands' print budgets and went to every major magazine and newspaper and asked for much larger discounts and more favorable treatment in exchange for a corporate schedule guarantee.

For example, General Motors consolidated the budgets for Chevrolet, Cadillac, Buick, GMAC, and all of their other entities and went to each publication of interest with a big pot of money.

It is important to understand that these advertisers created a win-win for the print media. The advertisers wanted large rate concessions and the media wanted more money and a commitment-- and knew that they would be shut out if they continued to be rigid about their rate cards.

That process changed everything. It is now quite possible to negotiate off-card rates and a variety of issues with print media (at least those who are living in the 21st century).

Print Negotiating Tips – Don't ask, don't get. Since print media can add and subtract pages on the basis of their sales, it is not as supply-and-demand sensitive as broadcast. However, newspaper sales and many magazine sales are soft. Always remember the power of the dollar: you have money, and they want it, or at least some of it. As long as that is true and you have a good Plan B in your pocket to use as leverage, there are opportunities to negotiate lower prices and added value.

1.   Caveat-Emptor – Media buyers beware. Media planning and buying can be a very confusing world. There are thousands of media, $300 billion in expenditures, massive amounts of research, computer systems, and media specialists. Further, the mission of every media rep is to sell you as many ads as possible at the highest possible price. Reps come up with very creative reasons and sheets of numbers why you should buy ads from them. They may even attempt to capitalize on the inexperience of a newbie. So your first order of business is to establish yourself as someone who knowledgeable and can't be snowed.

Ask each rep many questions about his/her publication. Ask what the circulation is and whether it is audited; what the rate base circulation is; how many readers they have, and according to what research; what are the demographics of the readers; what the publication's editorial purpose is; what research they have; what their page opening rates are, and other questions. Asking the rep good questions will help establish your credibility and let the rep know you are a knowledgeable buyer. Get this kind of information before you give the rep information on your target audience.

2. ***Take a Page from GM's Book*** – Go to the publications you are interested in using. Tell them you will increase your financial commitment with them IF they will give you a deep off-card discount. Make sure they know that you are looking for media who want a win-win relationship, and you will look elsewhere if they are not interested. (They would get NO business from you). Be prepared to walk away.

3. ***Study the Publication's Ads*** – Look at the publication in order to see how many "house" ads (promoting themselves) and/or public service ads they have. If they have a lot of non-revenue-producing ads, it may be a sign that they are having trouble selling advertising. **Buy low**.

4. ***Always Have a Plan B*** – If you are unable to negotiate the right deal with a particular publication(s), go to Plan B. Let the publication know you are taking the money somewhere else, and don't tell them where or when. If you receive no response, use the money to buy other media that are equally cost effective for your purposes.

5. ***Use Their Own Rate Card Against Them*** – When discussing rates with a magazine or newspaper that has a complex rate card, it is a good tactic to base your rate reduction rationale on some element of their card. For example, if you are planning to run 3-6 times, ask for the 12x rate. If they offer special rates to realtors or car dealers, ask for the dealer rate since you, too, are a dealer, just not a car dealer. Print media still like to stay on their card.

6. ***New Advertiser Discounts*** – Even the *New York Times* offers certain new advertisers deep discounts (e.g., 60-70%) based on an agreed-upon level of commitment.

7. ***Negotiate Value Added*** – Print media will also provide additional value at no added cost, e.g., reprints and point of sale, mailings to customers, copies of the publication to distribute at your place of business. You could ask them to conduct a sweepstakes or contest. You could ask them to host a golf outing for your clients. Be creative, but stick to things that fit your strategy!

8. *Get Free Exposure on Their Website* – Newspaper and magazine websites are growing in popularity. Ask that they give you links, ads, mentions on their website as part of their value added package.

9. ***Ask for Two Ads for the Price of One*** – Never forget: the newspaper business is soft. We have had success in getting two ads for the price of one. You might need to give the paper a commitment and some scheduling flexibility on the free ads.

10. ***Negotiate for Ad Positioning & Section of Publication*** – If it is a deal breaker for you, tell them so!

More Guerilla Buying Techniques

In addition to using leveraging strategies in negotiating media buys of traditional media, certain guerilla buying techniques can also offer a great opportunity get a lot more advertising time and space for the money. The following will discuss several techniques: buying remnants, online auctions & bidding platforms, pay per inquiry, pay per sale, and last but not least, media barter.

Media Remnants

The basis of remnant space advertising is that media companies rarely sell all of their advertising space. Their unsold ad space or time, called *remnant space*, can often be bought at steep discounts.

Like an unsold airline seat or hotel room, advertising time and space is a perishable commodity; if it is not sold, it is lost or given away for public service announcements or some other non-revenue producing filler. So, instead of taking a loss for unsold airtime or ad space, media outlets will often take far less than their usual retail fees to unload their remnant space. This means you can buy what is typically expensive media for much, much less than normal.

How you can best use remnant space advertising to your advantage depends upon the type of media in question:

Newspapers: Newspapers, because they are published daily and have a fairly set format, offer plenty of remnant space opportunities. One success factor, with newspapers especially, is your willingness to accept smaller remnant ads, because those are the ones that may be needed to fill out the paper. It also helps to have a good working relationship with your ad rep. Check out mss-standby.com.

Here's what another remnant supplier says: "Media Resources maintains an exclusive PaperTraxs® database of over 1,300 newspapers across the country, many of which offer guaranteed remnant rates exclusive to Media Resources. Because of Media Resources' strong newspaper relationships, we currently have an approximately 95% success rate in getting our client's ads in remnant/standby positions at these newspapers."

Some newspapers will put you on a "standby" program, where they hold an ad for you of a certain size, for a specified period of time. If they use it, you get it for, say, half price. If they don't use it, you are not billed naturally, but that's the risk you take—that it won't run. That's a direct route you could take, and even if your local paper doesn't have a formal arrangement like this, you may be able to work something out, particularly if the newspaper is locally owned.

Magazines: One of the great remnant opportunities lay with national magazines. Such magazines print regional editions and sell regional ads. If they fail to sell all of the regional ads (which is not uncommon), or sell an odd number, their unsold inventory is your opportunity.

But even smaller magazines offer remnant advertising. Magazines create their editorial content based upon, among other things, the amount of advertising sold. But sometimes advertisers back out, end up going with smaller ads, miss a deadline, or the magazine ends up with extra content, all of which creates an opportunity for you.

Radio: Radio is ripe for remnant buys because, unlike print media, which can be expanded and contracted to a certain extent as needed, radio advertising is finite; there are a fixed number of spots in one hour. Thus, getting that unsold time at "fire sale" prices is definitely doable. Discounts can range from 25 to 75% off retail prices.

One easy way to get remnant radio time is to buy regular time (at low negotiated prices). When you are ready to place an order, make the order contingent on their throwing in an equal number of remnant spots for free.

Television: The ever-expanding proliferation of television options—be they network, cable, or satellite—is also good news for the frugally minded entrepreneur. There is plenty of television remnant space to be had, and discounts can reach as much as 90% off the rate card.

An agency veteran handling smaller and mid-sized clients said of television: "Not really a big deal to big companies. They often do tons of TV advertising and have huge budgets to accomplish such. However, it's a really big deal for my clients— those companies of the small to mid-size. Why? Because there's a perception among advertisers and consumers that you're really successful if you can afford to advertise on TV."

If remnant space makes sense to you, one key is to make it easy for the media source to work with you and use your ad, and that means you have to be able to beat the "big boys." Because these ads come up at the last minute, media companies often would rather simply offer the opportunity to their larger advertisers because those advertisers have ready budgets, ad departments that can create an ad in a jiffy, and managers that can make a decision just about as quick. If you want these sorts of opportunities to come your way, then you have to be as viable and easy to work with as the large advertisers: First, let your ad rep know you are interested and ready, and second, earmark some money and have an ad ready to go.

Online: Most of the remnant advertising of big companies are sold to the ad networks such as BurstMedia, which in turn offers remnant advertising to their member publishers. There are also banner companies that approach publishers offering to buy their remnant ads. We've been approached several times by these companies, and often the rate is less than $1 CPM, where our banner ads go for $5 CPM.

So yes, remnant space can certainly stretch your advertising dollar, but just understand that it is not an easy way to advertise because it is so last minute. But if it does arise, you are in luck because it will certainly be cheap.

Online Media Auctions & Bidding Platforms

After a number of false starts, it appears that advertising auctions and ad bidding platforms are beginning to take off. A lot of the inventory these firms sell is remnants.

Bid4Spots.com – Bid4Spots.com is an online marketplace for radio stations to sell their unsold commercial inventory "easily and confidentially." It's a weekly reverse auction where radio stations (sellers) do the bidding for the advertiser's (buyer's) budget and spots selling for the lowest CPM (Cost per Thousand) win.

Mediabids.com – Mediabids.com is already the largest online auction/bidding house for print media. Advertisers can bid on available newspaper and magazine ad inventory or can initiate their own auction by making a bid for media not currently listed on the exchange.

Advertisers interested in bidding begin by selecting the market and circulation area, editorial focus, type of publication, and price point.

Mediabids.com then provides the availabilities in their system. Mediabids.com also provides a brief "media kit" on each of their media sponsors.

MediaBuys.com – **This** company positions itself as a "media buying club." To members, MediaBuys.com offers pre-discounted inventory in all media (claims 3,500 availabilities), including television, radio, magazines, and newspapers, all online.

MediaBuys.com claims savings of 10-60% vs. rate card prices. In addition, MediaBuys.com offers media planning and even creative assistance on a fee basis ($100 per hour). If the desired ad inventory is not in their ad bank, advertisers can fill out the campaign buys quote form and receive media space estimates from "thousands of competing media sources," claims MediaBuys.com. "Then, we return the lowest bids to online for your approval. If you like the quote, we buy the media on your behalf at the discounted rates."

RemnantRadio.com – Also called SoftWaveRadio.com, this bidding house solicits last minute inventory from radio stations. It promises buyers, "You can now buy spot radio in the markets you want, on the formats you select, targeting the demographic you choose. And, you can name your own price!"

"…It's an easy to use tool for purchasing spot radio locally, regionally, or nationally… without having to make a single phone call." (RemnantRadio.com)

eBay – Media auctions are the likely future of media buying. While its bid to start a live online auction for television was unsuccessful, an eBay auction house came very close to developing and implementing a $50 million test of a live online auctioning system. Spearheaded in 2006 by Wal*Mart and funded by a consortium of major advertisers (e.g., HP, Home Depot, Intel), the television auctioning system was to be developed and hosted by eBay, where advertising would be sold like other eBay goods

According to a press release from the Cable Advfertising Bureau (CAB), seven national cable networks tested the exchange, and executives at those networks decided it went too far in removing humans from the ad sales process—which put an end to the project. However, "The idea of media exchanges is gaining momentum," the marketers' group said in a statement. "We are still bullish about the system that has been produced." Stay tuned.

Google - Unlike the attempted advertiser/eBay foray into auctioning traditional media, Google has been doing deals with media companies which give Google a head start/toehold. Google will have live inventory to sell, and time to further develop its media and advertiser relationships and processes for testing and selling time and space on line. Some recent examples:

Google has inked a deal with EchoStar Communications and its 13.1 million satellite TV subscribers to sell and select some of the ads shown to, marking the online search leader's latest effort to extend its marketing muscle beyond the Internet. Google hopes to use this deal to prove that its automated system for online advertising can also be successfully applied to television.

"We think a lot of the principles of the Internet can be applied to the TV business," said Keval Desai, Google's TV product development director. So, will the EchoStar deal provide Google with the needed springboard into the $60+ billion market for broadcast & cable TV?

Clearly, in order to become a major player in the TV market, Google will have to extend its media relationships to include other satellite and cable TV providers, but Google has a nice start.

While Google's TV availabilities won't be as targeted as its online search terms, data from the set-top boxes of EchoStar subscribers will enable Google to tightly target certain demographics and geographics of EchoStar subscribers. Advertisers will pay only for the audience which was tuned to a commercial for some minimum time.

Google is also in the radio business. In addition to its acquisition of DMarc radio, Google has also signed a multi-year agreement with Clear Channel Radio (one of the largest radio station groups) which will allow Google to sell radio advertising on more than 675 of Clear Channel's stations. Under the agreement, Google Audio Ads advertisers will be able to reach specific audiences at specific times in targeted areas across the country.

"This is a true win-win," John Hogan, CEO of Clear Channel Radio, said in a statement. "Clear Channel Radio gets access to an entirely new group of advertisers within a new and complementary sales channel, and Google adds another option for its existing customers."

Clear Channel said the move is part of a larger initiative to differentiate its on-air ad inventory. The companies said the agreement complements an existing online advertising partnership in which Google provides text ads to Clear Channel's radio-station Web sites through the company's Online Music & Radio Unit.

Per Inquiry

Per-inquiry advertising is rather simple and straightforward. With conventional direct response advertising, you risk spending money without a guaranteed cost per response. Whereas with per inquiry, you are guaranteed to only pay a fixed, pre-negotiated cost per response. Under this plan, one PI firm would air your company's existing lead-generating commercial(s) on television networks/cable systems and radio stations at a mutually agreed upon, guaranteed fixed cost per lead. If your company does not have an existing commercial, PI firms can produce a professional, customized commercial to be used to generate lead flow for your company. Obviously, the attractive part of utilizing per inquiry advertising is that your company's "risk" will be dramatically reduced.

For example, if in the past, your company has aired a direct response commercial, then there is a specific cost per lead that you would have incurred. In other words, if you spent $10,000 on a radio campaign and you received a thousand (1,000) leads, your cost per lead would be $10. The same would air that same commercial at a mutually agreed upon, fixed cost per lead of approximately 20% less than the cost per lead you received through conventional media buying.

Pay Per Sale

Online Advertising – Google and a few others are testing a new online advertising payment model—pay per sale, a major development in the online advertising payment model in which payment is based solely based on qualifying sales. In a pay per sale agreement, the advertiser *only* pays for sales generated by the destination site based on an agreed upon commission rate.

Paying per sale is often seen as the payment model most favorable to advertisers and least favorable to publishers. In such an agreement, the publisher must not only be concerned with the quality and quantity of his or her audience, but also the quality of the advertiser's creative units and destination site.

If possible, some publishers avoid sales-based agreements, preferring to stick to the CPM model. However, some publishers, facing weak ad sales, have little choice but to accept sales-based agreements to utilize remnant space-- especially given Google as a competitor.

For advertisers, pay per sale has some unique advantages compared to pay per click and pay per lead. There are fewer concerns about whether conversions are legitimate and whether traffic is incentivized or of low quality.

Direct Response Opportunities – Other companies in the direct response advertising industry industries offer various forms of "pay per action" payment models using traditional advertising media.

Bartering for Media

For some small companies, bartering problem inventories for advertising/communications time and space can be a great guerilla media-buying tool. You can trade problem inventories or services gathering dust that would sell far below original wholesale or become write-downs.

You can barter for television, radio, print, internet or production of ads and commercials. You can barter for marketing/media consulting services, creative services, advertising specialty items—and more.

Media is a huge $300+ billion industry in the world today and is a "major currency" in the barter marketplace because of its perishability. One must use it, move it, or lose it. The second hand on the clock never stops. In this media section we look at many forms of media.

How Barter Works - No business attracts new customers without some form of advertising. From the *Yellow Pages*, to TV commercials, to cards on the church bulletin board, to "word of mouth" referrals, to the sign on your door, no customer comes to your business without first noticing you are there. Building a better mousetrap does not cause people to line up at your door...advertising the mousetrap does.

Through effective barter, you can trade excess inventory for advertising that will attract new cash customers. You can trade $2,000 worth of tires from your inventory for billboard exposure on the expressway that could generate thousands of dollars in new truck tire cash sales.

You can trade $3,000 worth of fax machines from your inventory for newscast radio advertising that could generate thousands of dollars in new fax machine sales.

You can trade $300 worth of pizzas for a mailing of 10,000 special offer coupons to homes in your area for generating the cash sales from hundreds of additional pizzas sold.

Can you trade for all of your advertising? Probably not. However, let's take a look at the cash you would save by trading for only 20% of your total ad budget.

Figure that at least 20% of your ad budget is variable. You try this...you impulse buy that. If you normally buy advertising on four local radio stations, how crucial is the 4th station? It may be essential to continue to buy the top two or three stations on a cash basis. But, it's likely you could trade for advertising on a different radio station which would be at least as effective as the fourth station on your list.

Let's say you spend 50% of your budget in the newspaper, 25% on television, and 25% on radio. Do you think it would hurt your overall advertising effectiveness to take just 4-5% away from each of these media?

Now, let's take that 12-15% and purchase billboard exposure through barter to give you a daily reinforcement of your other advertising. The result is, for the same budget, you are reaching the same people you always reach, plus new people through a new advertising source, and you were able to save money and cash flow by trading for a portion of your total program.

On a smaller scale, if you buy a 10" display ad in your strong local paper, you probably won't hurt effectiveness by cutting it down to an 8" ad. The same readers will see you week after week. Now, take that 20% and buy advertising in a strong local coupon mailer, multiplying your advertising's reach without increasing your budget...and barter for the coupon mailer. Don't be afraid to "play" with the variable portion of your ad budget.

You can almost always increase your reach without increasing your budget, and you can almost always replace at least 20% of your cash budget through barter. Many times, you can even do more.

If your co-op reimbursement is 75% or 100%, you're making money before the first customer walks in the door.

You can turn your barter credit into cash through co-op advertising. You can also turn your barter credit into cash through non co-op advertising. Trade exchanges that understand your ability to cash-convert through advertising can make a huge contribution to the positive cash flow of your business.

Direct Barter vs. Trade Exchanges - There are two ways to trade your products or services for media: go direct or go through a trade exchange.

First, you can contact media individually to see if they would be interested in a barter agreement. For example, if you own a nice restaurant, a station might trade some time (that they probably wouldn't sell anyway) for business lunches to wine and dine some important media buyers.

Second, you can work through a large trade exchange that has relationships with media and other types of companies. You can check to see if you have a local trade exchange in your city. Or you could choose to work with a larger barter exchange which may not have an office in your market. Large exchanges will have access to much more inventory than a small exchange.

If you choose to work with a trade exchange, you will have to pay a fee to join and a percentage of your transactions.

Contact barter exchanges which are compatible with your needs. Check out Barter News' website pages on bartering for media: http://www.barternews.com/how_to_barter_for_advertising.htm.

If you handle your own advertising, your trade exchange should have a qualified advertising representative who can help work barter into your advertising plan. If you work with an advertising agency, you should put it in touch with your trade exchange.

Have a "Cattle Call"

Another very effective technique for generating ideas and getting media to aggressively compete with each other is to stage a "cattle call" (at least that is what we called them).

You begin by developing a plan and guidelines defining for the media what you are looking for. Like a buying spec sheet, this document will define your objectives for the activity, your target market, timing, budget, creative guidelines, and the rationale for the request.

The next step is to request competitive media to develop turnkey media/promotion ideas for you for a special turnkey program of some kind, e.g., for a promotion. Media who wish to compete for your business will then develop their ideas, come up with a full package and costs, and come to see you/your team to present them.

Once you have seen all of the submissions, you will develop a short list of the two or three best ideas which best meet your guidelines and criteria. Then make your offers (changes in package, price, etc.), starting with your #1 preference. Buy one.

***

The guerilla media buying techniques described in Chapter 12 could increase your media purchasing power by 30-200%, depending on market conditions, techniques used, timing, and your skills. You can use guerilla buying (e.g., leveraging) successfully with traditional media, and you can turn to unconventional outlets for negotiating your buys as well

Chapter 13
Problems & Exercises

1. List and explain the media negotiating strategies discussed in Chapter 12. Why is win-win a central principle of successful negotiating? Why is developing leverage or an incentive for the seller so important?

2. List and explain 10 buying strategies for broadcast and print media which can result in more advertising exposure for the money.

3. Explain how each of the following guerilla buying techniques would or would not make sense for your business:

Guerrilla Negotiating -

Remnant Space:-

Auctions & Bidding -

Pay per Inquiry -

Pay per Sale -

Barter -

*"A medium is
"any extension of ourselves,
or more broadly,
any new technology."*

--Marshall McLuhan

Chapter 14
Setting a Budget to Grow By

How much should you spend in advertising or other marketing communications to increase your market share? The conventional wisdom suggests several ways to develop a budget.

A/S Ratio

The Advertising to Sales Ratio (A/S Ratio) is perhaps one of the most popular methods of arriving at an advertising budget. The A/S ratio for your industry will help you benchmark your spending against industry norms.

So, if a particular industry spends on average five% of sales on advertising, your budget would be five% of your sales, give or take any adjustments you might make to that average ratio. (Do you want to be higher or lower than average?) Knowing your A/S ratio can help you spend proportionately to competitors, although your particular situation may call for spending more or less. Recognizing that growth requires investment, the decision is ultimately yours.

There are two ways to arrive at a budget using A/S ratios. One is to use current year or last year's sales as the base. The second way would be to use your projected sales as a base. Let's assume last year's sales were $500,000 and your category's A/S ratio is 5%. Your budget would be $25,000 ($500,000 x .05). But if you are projecting sales to increase to $600,000 with a little help from more advertising, your budget would be $30,000.

The following table provides some general benchmarks. More detailed data can be found at www.dnb.com/us.

Advertising Sales Ratios, Selected Sectors

	A/S Ratio	% Sales Growth
Consumer Products	6.7	3.9
Health Care	4.3	3.8
Retail	1.8	5.4
Financial Svs.	1.2	7.1
Trans/Travel	2.0	.0
Services*	3.6	10.0
Wholesale	.6	3.9
Avg. Sector	**2.4**	**3.9**

* Except health care. Source: Schoenfeld Estimates, 2003

Even if you arrive at a budget by other means, comparing it to what your budget would be if based on your A/S ratio would provide a good logic check.

Task Method

In an ideal world, you would be able to accurately calculate how much it would cost to address each of the marketing or media tasks ahead of you. The total cost of the plans needed to address your various tasks would be your budget. However, to establish a budget using this method, you have to have clearly defined tasks and have an accurate method for determining the plan and spending needed to accomplish each.

Nevertheless, following are some simplified examples of how you might apply the task method.

Example 1 – Assume you sell an impulse purchase product sold in grocery and mass merchandising stores. You believe recency planning is the correct approach for your business. Therefore, you set a media objective of reaching 50% of your target every weeknight. That projects to 250 TRPS per week, approximately 13,000 TRPS per year. If the cost per TRP in your market averages $20 for the media you want, your budget would total $260,000. How does that budget compare to a budget developed by using the A/S ratio?

Example 2 – Assume you sell a considered purchase product such as computers. You believe you need monthly effective reach in traditional media and a heavy search presence on the internet (CPC). You calculate that you will need about 400 TRPS per month to effectively reach your target audience with traditional media. That totals 4800 TRPS per year at a cost per TRP of $20 in your market. For your media mix, your traditional media budget would be $96,000. In addition, generating 25,000 clicks on Google and Yahoo! will cost another $25,000 at an average of $1.00 per click. Your total budget would be $121,000 ($96,000 +$25,000).

Example 3 – Assume you have two key communications objectives and strategies for next year: 1) improve your image by implementing a PR and institutional advertising program, and 2) generate weekly store traffic with sales, offers, incentives communicated by mail and in the newspaper. The media and PR plan for the image-building program will cost $70,000, and the weekly traffic building mail/newspaper media plan will cost $150,000. The total budget would be $220,000.

Share Of Voice Goal

The third approach is to set a *SOV* goal in relation to your Share of Market goal for next year. This approach was discussed in Chapter 1.

To review, a great deal of research has found a high correlation between share of voice and share of market. You will recall that SOV is the percentage of category ad dollars your product or business represents.

SOV theory says that to maintain market share, share of voice should equal share of market, i.e., if your share of market is 10%, your share of voice should therefore be 10%.

SOV theory would also say that to grow market share next year, your share of voice should significantly lead your share of market goal. For example, if your current share of market is 10% , and your objective is to grow it to 12%, your share of voice would need to be 15-20%, i.e. every five messages exposed to the target market needs to be one of *yours*—in order to get the increased Share of Mind necessary to drive increased market share.

How do you determine your SOV is now?

As discussed Chapter 1, you (or someone you designate) have to call your sales reps from the relevant media vehicles in your geographic trading area and business segment, and have them ask the media how much each of your competitors spent with them in (time period). In most cases, the media will cooperate with you. You will likely have to estimate some dollars to fill in the gaps. Once you have all of the data, you can compile a table like this one:

Competitor	**Spend**	**SOV**
A	$30,000	30%
B	50,000	50
C	20,000	20
Total	**$100,000**	**100%**

How about *ESOV*? - Returning to the above example, if your current share of market is 10%, and your objective is to grow it to 12%, your Real SOV would need to be 18%.

If you are able to increase your ESOV by spending your dollars more efficiently and effectively, the out of pocket budget you need to achieve your ESOV goal would be reduced, potentially to zero.

Example 1
- Your business-building goal needs 18% SOV.
- If your current SOV is 10%, and you *conservatively* estimate a 50% improvement in spending effectiveness, your RSOV would be 15% without spending an extra dollar out of pocket.
- To reach 18% RSOV, you need to increase your budget by 30%.

Example 2
- Your business-building goal needs 18% SOV.
- If your current SOV is 10%, and you estimate a 100% improvement in spending effectiveness, your RSOV would be 20% without spending an extra dollar out of pocket.
- To reach—and exceed 18% RSOV—you would not need to increase your budget at all!

Allocating Your Budget

Regardless of the method you use to arrive at your total media budget, you will also have to decide how to most effectively allocate it among various forms of marketing communications, products, departments, time of year, and so on.

Nobody can anticipate everything that could happen over the course of the year. (Yogi Berra: "We don't know what we don't know.")We suggest retaining a contingency reserve in your budget to address unforeseen problems or opportunities and to capitalize on great buying opportunities when they arise.

For the same reason, we also suggest that you maintain a fairly high degree of flexibility in your budget. You need to be able to reallocate dollars if the marketplace warrants it.

Finally, the ideal budget development process would utilize all of the methods we have briefly outlined so that you can better judge the rationality of the results.

The key to building Share of Market is to ensure that your ESOV significantly leads your Share of Market goal. For example, if you want to increase your Share of Market from 15% to 20%, your ESOV would need to be 30-40% or more.

You start by measuring your current SOV and estimate how much improvement you can achieve in planning and buying.

Chapter 14
Review

1. Calculate what your marketing communications budget would be on the basis of your sector's A/S ratio:

	This Year	Next Year
Sales		
A/S Ratio		
Budget		

2. List your basic marketing tasks for next year, and identify a plan and budget requirement to execute it:

	Task	Plan	Cost
1.			
2.			
3.			

3. What is your Share of Market vs. SOV goal for next year?

	This Year	Next Year
Total Spending		
SOV Goal		
ESOV Goal		
Share of Market		
Budget Needed		

On Winning

*"Winning isn't everything,
it's the only thing."*

--Vince Lombardy

\

Chapter 15
Winning!

$$ESOV = SOV + QOV$$

Effective Share of Voice has two components: Share of Voice (messages) and the Quality of Voice(quality of messages). Taken together, these two factors can help small businesses look more important, more successful, and more credible to consumers who currently buy from Goliath.

*The purpose of this book was to teach small business leaders how to use a new business building model which can increase ESOV, market share, and profit. Key conceptual and tactical skills were presented to help small business owners and entrepreneurs **implement their own plan or provide direction to others.***

Your Path to Success

If you are inexperienced in media, the path to success will require effort. But if you are successful in following the path, the payback will be great. Here are the distilled steps:

*1.   **Get to Know Media*** – Develop an understanding of media concepts, terminology, planning, buying, and analysis/media math so that you can more effectively collect and analyze relevant information, plan, buy, and negotiate with sellers.

*2.   **Build a Strong Strategic Marketing Platform*** – A strategic marketing plan is just as important for small business as large business, if not more so. Your media plan will be affected by your marketing objectives and strategies, problems and opportunities.

*3.   **Understand Your Bag of Marketing Communications Tools*** – Advertising, the web, public relations, direct marketing, sponsorships and events so that you can impact the market most successfully and cost effectively. Advertising doesn't do everything!

*4.   **Reach & Communicate with Your Target Audiences*** – Focus on your priorities of current customers and tier one prospects. Understand who they are, what motivates them, what their buying process is.

*5.   **Spend Your Ad Dollars in Your Primary Marketing Area*** – Minimize spending outside your market area so that you can maximize impact on your most likely buyers and maximize your ROI.

*6.   **Evaluate and Select the Right Media for the Job*** – Do your homework and analysis. Make media decisions based on facts and good judgment, not emotion. The task is to most effectively reach and communicate with your target audiences.

*7.   **Use the Internet to Further Level the Playing Field*** – You can look like a leading corporation on the internet. Consider e-commerce for direct sales and lead generation.

*8.   **Negotiate Traditional Media Buys at 30-60%+ Savings*** – Use the buying strategies and techniques in the book to negotiate both broadcast and print buys. Reinvest the savings into more Share of Voice.

*9. **Use Guerilla Media Buying Techniques*** – Save up to 50-60% or more by utilizing a variety of non traditional media buying techniques e.g., auctions & bidding platforms, buy remnants in all media, barter for media time & space, try pay per inquiry and pay per sale to see if it is cost effective for you.

*10. **Think Outside the Traditional Media Box*** – Consider a range of low cost, effective non-traditional media/communications ideas that can give you even more bang for the buck exclusively in your trading area (no waste). We've included some thought starters in the book.

*11. **Quality of Voice*** – In order to conquest customers of larger businesses, you must appear to be a quality concern, we assume you are. Therefore, in addition to message weight and media effectiveness, your creative must also be of high quality. Your website, ads, newsletters, publicity, direct mail, and everything else must be highly professional, reflecting a first class image for your company.

*12. **Budget to Win*** – Make sure your budget is adequate to achieve ESOV which is at least 50% higher than your Share of Market goal.

Your Leverage

What you can realistically achieve in terms of eliminating waste from your spending and increasing the cost efficiency and effectiveness of your spending is up to you. If you follow the suggestions made in this book, there is no doubt that you can increase your Effective Share of Voice without increasing your out of pocket budget.

Example 1 - Let's consider the following hypothetical, conservative situation where spending yielded an additional 100% lift in weight by capturing the agency commission and cash discount, combined with more effective & targeted media planning (very conservative), use of some non-traditional media, and a range of opportunistic media buying techniques.

Example 1	% Budget	% Improve.	Wtd. % Improve.
Capture Agency Commission	100	15	15
Capture Cash Discount	50	2	1
Effectiveness of Plan	100	30	30
Non Traditional Media	10	30	3
Media Buying	50	40	20
Remnants	10	50	5
Barter	20	60	12
Auctions/Bidding	20	50	10
Other	20	25	4
	100	-	+100

If you realized a 100% increase in spending effectiveness, you would increase your ESOV by up to 100%—barring unlikely heavy competitive reactions to a stealth shift in strategy.

Example 2 - If you were also able to also significantly improve the effectiveness of your media plan, perhaps because it had allocated so much money outside your primary market area, the increase in media weight could be much greater, in this example, an increase of 170%,

Example 2	% Budget	% Improve.	Wtd. % Improve.
Capture Agency Commission	100	15	15
Capture Cash Discount	50	2	1
Effectiveness of Plan	100	100	100
Non Traditional Media	10	30	3
Media Buying	50	40	20
Remnants	10	50	5
Barter	20	60	12
Auctions/Bidding	20	50	10
Other	20	25	4
	100	-	+170

Clearly, by following this model, you have an opportunity to potentially increase your ESOV significantly.

***

Advertising legend, Leo Burnett, once said, "If you reach for the stars, you might not quite catch one, but you won't come up with a hand full of mud either."

So it is with fighting Goliath for market share. You might not bring the giant to his knees, but you can sure hit him in the head with a large, hard rock by faithfully implementing the strategies and ideas found in this book.

*The purpose of this book has been to provide small businesses with **a new way to win**. Provided that you already do a great job of meeting a consumer need with a strong value proposition, how much you can increase your market share by increasing ESOV is up to you.*

In addition, different small businesses will apply the strategies and techniques found in this book in different ways.

For example, a business with a budget of $5,000 or less would likely focus on ways to leverage exposure at little or no cost, e.g., frequent publicity releases, newsletters, cross promotions with complementary businesses, product placement—compared to a much larger business with a large budget who is able to benefit across the board

Happy Giant Hunting!

***

Chapter 15
Review

1.Set your targets by category (based on your business situation)

	% Budget	% Improve.	Wtd. % Improve.
Capture Agency Commission			
Capture Cash Discount			
Effectiveness of Plan			
Non Traditional Media			
Media Buying			
Remnants			
Barter			
Auctions/Bidding			
Other	20		
	100	100	

2.Develop a plan for each target area:

	Strategy 1	Stategy 2	Strategy 3
Agency Comm.			
Effectiveness			
Non Trad. Med.			
Media Buying			
Remnants			
Barter			
Auctions/Bids			

WINNING!

THE END

Books From
2020:Marketing Communications LLC

▪▪ı

David vs. Goliath, Guerrilla Media Buying for Small Business, 2007

Free Marketing in Social Media: 500 Tactics & Best Practices, 2010

Unique International Recipes, 2010

Guerrilla Media Buying for Small (and Large) Business, 2010

Bibliography

Abratt, R. , and P. S. Grober. "The Evaluation of Sports Sponsorship." International Journal of Advertising 8 (1989): 351-62.

Baker, David, Share of Voice and Other Vital Metrics, 2007

Eisenhart, Tom. "Telemarketing Takes Quantum Leap." Business Marketing. September 1993.

Davis, John, "Magic Numbers for Consumer Marketing," 2005

Everett, Martin. "It's Jerry Hale on the Line." Sales & Marketing Management. December 1993.

Geskey, Ronald D., *David vs. Goliath: Guerrilla Media Buying for Small Business, a New Way to Win*, 2007

Geskey, Ronald D. *Free Marketing in Social Media: 500 Tactics and Best Practices,* 2010

Geskey, Ronald D., *How to Really Buy Spot* TV, AdMediaStore.com, ed. 2, 2007

Geskey, Ronald D. Media 101, AdMediaStore.com, ed. 2, 2007

Geskey, Ronald D, 2007 Thumbnail Media Planner, 2020:Marketing Communications LLC 2007.

Geskey, Ronald D. Strategic Media Planning, 2020:Marketing Communications LLC 2007.

Geskey, Ronald D., Recency Planning: Revisited, AdMediaStore.com, 2005

Geskey, Ronald D., Effective Reach: Revisited, AdMediaStore.com, 2005

Gottlieb, Mag. "Telemarketing and the Law." Direct Marketing. February 1994.

Hudson, Adams. "The Dos and Don'ts of Direct Mail Marketing." Air Conditioning, Heating, and Refrigeration News. October 23, 2000.

Hudson, Adams. "How to Select the Most Profitable Direct Mail List." Air Conditioning, Heating, and Refrigeration News. November 20, 2000.

Kernak, Al., Putting Your Business Online, Ed. 2, 2005

Kleinman, Mark. "Why the Future of Media Is Direct." Marketing. November 16, 2000.

Kobs, Jim. Profitable Direct Marketing. 2nd ed. NTC Business Books, 1992.

Lewis, Herschell Gordon. Direct Marketing Strategies and Tactics. Dartnell, 1992.

Lister, Gwyneth J., Building Your Direct Mail Program, Jossey-Bass, 2001.

McHatton, Robert J. Total Telemarketing. Wiley, 1988.

McLuhan, Robert. "Warm Calling Builds Results." Marketing. August 5, 1999.

Miller, Rachel. "Getting Big Results from a Small Spend." Marketing. September 7, 2000.

Moretti, Peggy. "Telemarketers Serve Clients." Business Marketing. April 1994.

Rice, C. Marketing Without a Marketing Budget, Bob Adams, 1999.

Rosen, Judith. "Telemarketing: Pros and Cons." Publishers Weekly. January 11, 1999.

Samli, A. Up Against the Retail Giants, Thomson, 2004

Schultz, Don & Barnes, Beth (1995). Strategic advertising campaigns, 4th ed. Lincolnwood, IL: NTC Publishing.

Schultz, Don & Tannenbaum, Stanley I. (1988). Essentials of advertising strategy. Lincolnwood, IL: NTC Publishing

Sissors, J. and Baron, R. Advertising Media Planning, 6th Ed, McGraw Hill, 2002

Stone, Bob. Successful Direct Marketing Methods. 4th ed. NTC Business Books, 1989.

Scott, Howard. "Targeting Prospects with Direct Mail." Nation's Business. September 1997.

Toth, Debora. "Direct Mail: Still Marketing's Darling." Graphic Arts Monthly. September 2000.

www.ingramcontent.com/pod-product-compliance
Lightning Source LLC
Chambersburg PA
CBHW071545080326
40689CB00061B/1824